MAKING A TEAM WORK

Making a Team Work

How to Lead a Team Effectively

STEVE CHALKE
with
Penny Relph

KINGSWAY PUBLICATIONS
EASTBOURNE

ISBN 0 85476 453 4

Designed and produced by
Bookprint Creative Services
P.O. Box 827, BN21 3YJ, England for
KINGSWAY PUBLICATIONS LTD
Lottbridge Drove, Eastbourne, E. Sussex BN23 6NT.
Printed in Great Britain.

Contents

Introduction

The ability to build, mobilise and maintain a team is an essential quality for any effective, long-term leader. Why? Because 'Lone Ranger' leadership – however it's disguised, packaged or justified – will never be effective in building the local church or, for that matter, any lasting organisation.

A local church functions best only when it truly becomes what it is intended to be: a body, or team, of committed volunteers and paid employees working together to support one another and to achieve a set of common goals. But the concept of teamwork is not only thoroughly biblical, it's also sensible and practical.

The effectiveness of any team depends on the quality of its leader. We tend to use the term 'great leader' too often and too lightly. A great leader isn't someone we all stand in awe of. A truly great leader is someone who builds a team and inspires others to do well; not someone who leaves you believing in *them* so much as believing in *yourself* and your own abilities. The ultimate test of a great leader is therefore not so much what happens when they're around but what happens when they're gone. Will their work continue or fall apart?

That is the challenge I face as a church leader and founder of the Oasis Trust, an organisation concerned with evangelism and social action, based in London and working both in the UK and around the world. My aim is not that people will be impressed with what I do but rather that they will be trained and inspired to do better themselves. So my goal is that the preachers within Oasis will be equipped to preach better than I can; the communicators to communicate more effectively than I have; and the planners to plan more strategically and thoroughly. My overall goal is to leave Oasis stronger not weaker when I am gone.

So many of us involved in church leadership have had little or no training in team management skills. I studied theology as I prepared for the Baptist ministry, but left college with little or no understanding of what it took to lead a congregation. I found myself thrown in the deep end and sinking fast. All that I have subsequently learned about leadership and making a team work has been learned as Oasis has grown and as I have pastored various churches. Therefore, this book has been written specifically with the needs of the local church in mind. Although it deals with many management skills it also looks beyond them to examine the character of the leader – recognising that Christian leadership always begins with who you are, not what you do.

But don't make the mistake of thinking *Making a Team Work* is only for pastors and elders; it's written for everyone with responsibility within a local church. While the effective church is one big team, at the same time it also comprises many smaller teams dedicated to specific aspects of the group's life – eg, youthwork, evangelism, social action, children's work, finance, administration and worship. Whatever aspect of your church's ministry you are involved in, it is vital that you understand and apply the principles of teambuilding.

Take note, this is not a book to be read and then left on the shelf to gather dust. It is designed to be studied and then applied to your team and situation. It is designed to lead you through the principles of effective team leadership and then to help you apply them through a variety of exercises, assessments and checklists. *Making a Team Work* can be used by individuals, be worked through in a group context, and even adapted to form the basis for your own training day.

Although this book is written primarily with the local church in mind, the same principles apply in business, in voluntary work and to community projects; in fact, to all team situations whenever and wherever they occur.

SECTION 1

The Importance of Teamwork

*'The absence of teamwork at any level
will limit organisational effectiveness and
can eventually kill an organisation.'*
Robert B. Maddux

Why build a team?

Teamwork makes sense! It's the logical way to achieve your task at the same time as giving other people the opportunity to develop their gifts and skills.

Teamwork is productive. It is a tried and tested way of getting things done. The benefits of co-operating with others to achieve a common goal are self-evident. A good team reacts more quickly, moves faster and can actually achieve far more than the sum of the individuals that make it up.

The story of Nehemiah in the Old Testament is a prime example of this. While living in exile, Nehemiah had a dream to rebuild the walls of Jerusalem. Gaining permission from King Artaxerxes, he set off to Jerusalem and rode round the city on a donkey to survey the job. He then divided all the people of the city into teams so that every family had a part to play in the task. Despite great opposition, Nehemiah and his team achieved their goal. What others had failed to do in seventy years, Nehemiah got done in just fifty-two days because he deployed a whole team.

Sadly, thousands of years later, too many church leaders have failed to learn from Nehemiah's lesson. Without a team of co-workers, any leader's ability to achieve anything of lasting value, however talented they are, will be very limited, and the vast pool of potential in local churches will remain untapped.

Teamwork is creative. Although we usually assume that our way is the best, we all know that there is usually more than one way to achieve a goal. A good team will generate stronger and more creative ideas and produce more imaginative solutions to problems than are likely to result from the best efforts of a single mind. The best kind of team is therefore one that represents a diversity of opinion. If you surround yourself with others who are guaranteed always to agree with you, the inevitable result will be mediocrity. Creativity is born out of the tension of differing opinions, approaches and insights.

As iron sharpens iron, so one man sharpens another.

(Prov 27:17)

But no team should exist purely to fulfil a set of tasks.

Teamwork builds character. A team also provides an excellent environment for personal development. The opportunity to work alongside other people within a supportive framework is one which allows individuals to develop their skills and to realise their potential. It provides a safe, secure environment where mistakes can be made without losing face and it also provides a positive context for exposing and dealing with those rough edges that quickly become apparent when the pressure is on!

Teamwork produces new leaders. A good team provides the ideal environment in which to identify and train future leaders. One of the greatest priorities of any thinking leader is to ensure the stability of the group under the next generation of leaders.

One of the first things Jesus did when he began his ministry was to gather together what others might have viewed as a rather second-rate bunch of misfits to mould into the team which he would train and ultimately trust to continue his work. Jesus made it a major priority to invest time in developing future leaders of the church.

Teamwork promotes a sense of belonging. As John Donne said, 'No man is an island.' Every human being has the basic need to belong. The lack of 'belonging', and the sense of insecurity and isolation that results from this, is a root cause of much of our society's breakdown. Being part of a team can bring a sense of both identity and security, so important to human development and fulfilment.

Back to basics

The fact that teamwork makes economical, creative, psychological, strategic and social sense is true primarily because that's the way God made us and intends us to work.

Teamwork is biblical. In the New Testament, the word 'church' literally means a 'called out' people or society. In fact, originally it was also used to describe other associations of people joined together by a common purpose. So its very name indicates that the church was never intended to function as a loose collection of individualistic, independent players. It was always supposed to be an *interdependent* team, recognising and benefiting from each of its members' gifts, strengths and abilities.

The true meaning of the word 'church' is underlined by the apostle Paul when he describes it as the 'body of Christ'.

Just as each of us has one body with many members,
and these members do not all have the same function,
so in Christ we who are many form one body, and each
member belongs to all the others.   (Rom 12:4–5)

Of all places, the local church should be the one where teamwork is modelled at its best!

A team:

■ Provides the only effective means to enable a leader to achieve lasting goals and establish projects that will stand the test of time.

■ Generates a high level of creative and innovative ideas which result from the interaction of its members.

- Provides a large pool of talent and skills which can be deployed to the best overall advantage.

- Provides the environment to identify and train future leaders.

- Increases its members' sense of involvement, belonging and commitment to various projects and areas of ministry.

What makes a good team?

In all sorts of circumstances and situations, people form groups. But a group of people is not necessarily a team. The word 'team' was originally applied to a row of oxen or horses harnessed together, when it was discovered that they pulled better that way. Our use of the word today stems from those teams of animals. In other words, a team is a unit, in which every member's task is to pull their own weight in the same direction and at the same time. Within it, each member understands that their input is vital to the overall success, and is therefore motivated to use their individual abilities to benefit the unit as a whole.

A group does not become a team simply because it calls itself a team. There are a great many so-called 'teams' which are really nothing more than a number of individuals thrown together. Consider your own team. Is it really working together as a tight unit? Can you identify with the following?

One purpose   We understand our common goals and that they are best accomplished together, with mutual support. We do not work at cross purposes.

Involvement   Rather than being told what to do, we are free to suggest ways in which things might be done and to apply our particular talents in achieving team objectives.

Communication We are able to be honest and open with each other, and we always make an effort to understand different points of view.

Trust We encourage each other to express ideas, disagreements and feelings, with the confidence that expressions of opinion are not considered to be divisive or non-supportive.

Training We emphasise good training and create opportunities for members to develop their abilities with the full support and encouragement of the rest of the team.

Commitment We have a common sense of 'ownership' for the team's goals. We are all loyal to each other and committed to the team as a whole.

If a team is working well, all of the above statements will be true. If not, then adjustments to improve matters will increase the team's sense of purpose and unity as well as its productivity.

What makes a good leader?

A team is only as good as its leader. Even the most talented and motivated group of people will be severely limited in their effectiveness if they are not well led.

There are probably as many theories about leadership as there have been leaders. In fact, it seems as though almost every man or woman of influence has left behind them umpteen volumes of pithy quotes on the subject! In a world filled with so much conflicting advice, it is vital that we avoid merely swallowing the opinions of the latest 'expert'.

Our society tends to judge a leader on the array of his gifts and abilities. For instance, the leader of a local church is often considered to be the one who is (or at least should be!) better at preaching, teaching, pastoring or evangelism than the majority of the congregation.

In the New Testament, however, Paul's concept of leadership is quite different. He describes leaders not as those who do everything themselves, but as those who use their gifts and abilities to equip other people

> *to prepare [literally, to bring to a state of readiness]*
> *God's people for works of service, so that the*
> *body of Christ may be built up. . .*

(Eph 4:12)

Paul's own ministry was focused to this end, always encouraging others and pleased when they did things well. Recognition by others was simply a by-product of this calling.

A team coach

A church leader's most important job, therefore, is to train and mobilise every member of their congregation. A leader may well be a gifted preacher, evangelist or teacher, but the focus of their role is to equip other people. In fact, they might not excel in *any* of those areas, but if they have the ability to equip others, they will be a better leader than someone who is impressive on a stage but, in the final analysis, only leaves people impressed with their ability rather than equipped to do the job themselves. The biggest question to ask of anyone who claims to be a leader is, Do they leave me believing in their ability or do they introduce me to my own ability?

In a football team there may be a great many talented players, but the team's success will ultimately depend on the coach's ability to recognise the particular strengths and weaknesses of each player and train them to work together. The coach is not the star, of course, and is judged only by how the team performs *as a team*. Yet their guidance and input is the key element.

Qualities of an effective team leader

Good leadership is fundamentally about qualities and attitudes. In other words, it's not so much about what you do as who you are. Character was the first qualification the early church looked for in choosing its leaders.

- Good leadership means having a **clear vision**. A leader is always going somewhere, never satisfied with simply maintaining the status quo; their task is to engage the future creatively. It has been said that people generally fall into two groups – those who mould the future and those who are moulded by it. Leaders belong to the first category. They also need to have vision for those they lead, inspiring and challenging them, in order to draw the best out of them.

- Good leadership will involve possessing **the willingness to delegate**. A team leader needs to change their focus from doing a job well to equipping others to do it – perhaps even better.

- All leaders handle power, and none are exempt from the temptation to use it to satisfy their own ends. But good leadership will always involve **the use of power** to serve rather than dominate.

- Good leadership will also include the vital qualities of **trustworthiness** and **accountability**.

These qualities are considered in Section 2 of this book.

Skills of team leadership

An effective leader is more than a skilled manager. Management is essentially the stewardship of resources. It is concerned with making a group of people or an organisation work effectively and efficiently. But while leadership is more than management, an effective team leader must be able to lead and to manage. There are certain skills that play a key role in developing the potential both of a leader and their team.

- Important skills include **communicating** a vision to people in an effective way and **motivating** them to work together. A leader also needs to know how to go about **choosing a team** which will be appropriate for a particular project or area of work.

- Setting **goals and objectives** is essential for progress, as is knowing how to work towards them systematically and consistently. And any big goals will never be achieved without understanding and applying the practice of **delegation**.

- **Making decisions** is part of the job of any team leader, and is a skill which can be learned, bringing great benefit to the health and life of any team.

All of these skills are considered in Section 3 of this book.

Working together

Having great leadership qualities and knowing how to manage a team to achieve a goal are very important, but teamwork is about developing *people* as well as achieving *tasks*. An understanding of how to bring out the best in individuals and the team as a whole will make the difference between a good team and a great one.

- Good leadership involves putting **people before projects**, so that nobody ends up feeling 'used'. It involves helping your team members achieve their full potential by practical **training for success**.

- Of course, teamwork will never be without occasional areas of disagreement. **Understanding and resolving conflict** will help you minimise any destructive effects.

- **Building commitment** in a team will mean that people will really enjoy their work.

These interpersonal aspects of teamwork are considered in Section 4 of this book.

Time to act

Section 5 will help you to develop a personal action plan for improving your ability to lead a team effectively.

What kind of leader are you?

The first step forward in terms of improving your leadership qualities and skills is to develop a realistic picture of exactly where you are at the moment. Most of us assume we are easy-going, that we give a clear sense of direction to all who work with us and that we manage others well. But is it true? How well are you actually doing? The following questionnaire is designed to help you evaluate what kind of leader you really are.

Me and my team

Give a photocopy of the following blank questionnaire to someone who knows you well, and whose opinion you trust – perhaps another leader or, better still, a member of your team. Get them to fill it in honestly, answering according to their assessment of you (preferably while you are not around!).

Fill in another copy yourself, separately, and compare the results. How well do you know your own strengths and weaknesses, and do others see you the same way? Remember, this is an exercise in self-appraisal, not self-defence. It is important to be truthful.

Read each statement below and score:

    3 – if you're strong in that area;

2 – if you're average;
1 – if you're weak and
0 – if, to be honest, you're useless.

1. I am clear about the overall purpose of the team. ☐

2. I give team members a sense of ownership by involving them in setting goals for our work, and I place a high priority on listening to their ideas and views. ☐

3. We have regular team meetings to assess our progress. ☐

4. I provide the environment for an open discussion of problems, and encourage solutions to be found corporately. ☐

5. I am willing to admit my mistakes and to change my mind. ☐

6. My team knows that I trust and respect them. ☐

7. My team knows that I appreciate the work they do. ☐

8. I give praise and recognition to individuals publicly for their achievements on a regular basis. ☐

9. I give praise and recognition to individuals privately for their achievements on a regular basis. ☐

10. I am aware of my team's personal commitments outside the life of the team. ☐

11. I understand that conflict within any team is normal, but I work to resolve it quickly, and before it becomes destructive. ☐

12. I am good at spotting talent and latent ability in others. ☐

13. I am always ready to delegate authority. ☐

14. I work hard to provide opportunities to stretch and challenge team members and to help them develop new skills. ☐

15. I discuss a team member's performance with them at least every six months. ☐

16. I make sure that team members have access to information and training necessary for them to do their job effectively. ☐

17. I talk with team members honestly and openly, and encourage the same kind of communication in return. ☐

18. I enjoy working with other people. ☐

19. I get on well with the other members of the team on a personal basis. ☐

20. I encourage the team to think and act like a team by supporting one another. ☐

21. I have a good track record for keeping volunteer team members. ☐

22. I lead by setting high standards and a good example. ☐

TOTAL SCORE: _____

Analysis

55+ You are a skilled team builder, but there is always room for improvement. You have the kind of positive attitude towards other people that is essential in building and maintaining a strong team. But, before congratulating yourself too heartily, you would be wise to get the results back from your friend's assessment.

44–54 You have great potential, but need to keep working hard to become a really effective team builder.

27–43 It's time you did some very serious thinking about the way in which you handle other people. Don't make excuses; it's up to you to put in some determined effort.

Less than 27 Don't despair, leadership skills can be *learned*. How did your colleague score you? Maybe you are just too humble! But if they scored you around the same mark, urgent action is needed. Remember the famous words of the Sandhurst Commanding Officer who informed one of his recruits, 'You're not a born leader yet, but we're working on it!'

SECTION 2

Qualities of an Effective Team Leader

*'Your attitudes are far more fundamental
to your success in teambuilding than
any skill or techniques.'*
John Adair

Clear vision

Vision is spawned by faith, sustained by hope, sparked by imagination and strengthened by enthusiasm. It is greater than sight, deeper than a dream, broader than an idea.

Charles Swindoll

Of the many characteristics that are essential to Christian leadership, vision is the most important. Others, such as servanthood, are of course crucial, but should in reality be the hallmark of every Christian. It is primarily their sense of vision which sets leaders apart from those they lead. Vision, the ability to see beyond what is, to what should be, is the very essence of leadership. The health of every local church depends on it. As Solomon pointed out, 'For lack of guidance, a nation falls' (Prov 11:14).

The task of every team leader is to possess, articulate and communicate a compelling vision that will enable their team to set its sights on and invest its energy in future possibilities. Without vision, you can *manage* a team but you can't *lead* it anywhere. Leadership without vision is doomed to mediocrity and therefore, ultimately, to failure.

Movements and monuments

In his book *Christian Leadership*, John Perry writes, 'Sadly, many Christian leaders end up without any vision or even real

26

desire for it. They had vision once in the past, but now are content to rest on the laurels of past achievements.' One of the saddest aspects of church history is the many stories of exciting movements which ended as monuments. Still today, we all know of many churches and organisations which bear exactly the same hallmarks. The pattern:

A man (or woman) with an exciting vision sets off on a mission which inspires a following. As it gathers momentum, it becomes:

A movement. As it grows larger and more successful, structures are put into place which are essential to contain the growth. But slowly a subtle shift begins to take place. The energy of the organisation begins to be spent more on maintenance than pioneering. The leadership style becomes more concerned with the management of what exists than moving onto new ground. In reality the young movement has now become inflexible and slow-moving. It has become:

A machine which eventually grinds to a halt. Unfortunately this process sometimes lasts many years! Some organisations are kept alive in a persistent vegetative state by a few enthusiasts who fail to recognise that real life has long gone. When a movement stops moving, it inevitably becomes nothing more than:

A monument to its own past, existing only to exist. It is preoccupied with looking back to glorious days of past success and achievement but devoid of all understanding of today or direction for the future.

Starting a movement is relatively easy. Keeping it on the move is much harder because human beings are creatures of habit with a tendency to settle, and because without fresh challenges they will become set in their ways. However, if a movement is to stay alive, it must be continually moving from one adventure to another. For this reason, a sense of vision is an essential asset for every effective leader.

The writing on the wall

These are some of the danger signs of a church or organisation at risk of becoming a monument:

- The original leaders are reluctant to stand aside for new ones coming through the ranks.
- Leaders feel content with things as they are – there is no sense of frustration about what could be.
- People tend to talk more about the past than the future.
- Any proposed changes are treated with suspicion.

Characteristics of vision

A visionary leader is future-oriented. While most people are focused on the job in hand, the leader should be planning the next step. A leader's task is to see the opportunities and possibilities, and so work to shape the future rather than allowing events and circumstances to shape them. A leader should be an architect of the future, not its victim.

Being future-oriented will prevent a leader from becoming overwhelmed by immediate problems. In the middle of inevitable difficulties they will have the capacity to focus on finding solutions and moving on.

A visionary leader is going somewhere. They are always on a journey, moving from the security of the present into the 'undiscovered country' of the future, leading the way. Although the details of their long-term goal will rarely be clear, they must have a strong sense of direction and constantly be on the move. After all, if you aren't going anywhere, how can anyone follow you?

A visionary leader has a sense of purpose. The picture that the New Testament paints of Jesus is far removed from the modern-day caricature of a first-century hippy rambling around Galilee with a bunch of country bumpkins! Instead, Jesus strides across the stage of history with a highly-developed sense of destiny. The

Gospels demonstrate that, even in his death, far from being a victim of circumstances, Jesus was ultimately the architect of both the events and their timing.

A visionary leader is dependent on God. If Jesus' life was marked by a sense of destiny, it was also characterised by his dependence on his Father for the daily outworking of that purpose. He constantly made time to withdraw from the crowds to sharpen his sense of guidance and direction and to receive new strength. Jesus' public life was built around periods when he could be alone and listen to his Father. His example shows us that we too have to learn how to retreat in order to advance. It is a wise leader who places high priority on giving sufficient time for God to direct the thoughts and plans that give their vision its substance and are essential in keeping it fresh and alive.

A visionary leader is not distracted. To lead a team well it's important to keep your focus on the 'big picture' rather than allowing yourself to become totally submerged in the daily demands and details of life. If a leader reaches the point where they are being controlled by the pressures around them, they are failing in their prime task. A leader is called to be 'pro-active' as well as 'reactive'. The goal is to maintain a balance between the inevitable pull of the 'urgent' and the vital but threatened task of finding time to focus on the 'important'. Achieving this may involve the sacrifice of some worthy, but non-essential, aspects of their work. It may also mean taking some unpopular decisions. But, for failure to address this issue, many have ended up surviving rather than leading.

A visionary leader is consistent. A foolproof method of sapping the motivation of even your most enthusiastic team member is to head off in one direction this week and another next week. Although, as a leader, you will be constantly involved with change and adjustments, it's the consistency of your decisions and your direction which will enable people to put their confidence in your ability to judge what is really important.

A visionary leader is courageous. It's always easier to retread old ground and do things the tried and tested way. Unfortunately, courage doesn't become any easier with experience. In fact, the larger and more successful your team, church, or organisation becomes, the more is at stake, and so the temptation to play safe and settle for what you've got increases. So many people begin as radicals but, as the years pass, slowly settle for a tomorrow which looks and feels like yesterday.

A visionary leader works hard. Contrary to popular belief, it also takes hard work to be a visionary. It may be true that vision is born out of dreaming about the future, but it is equally the case that it arises from a realistic assessment of the resources available and the problems to be faced. The basic equation is:

$$Dreams + Reality = Vision$$

Clear vision results from the powerful mix of dreams and reality. And it's through the disciplines of constant prayer, reading, observation, talking, asking, listening and debating, that a leader is able to gather together the essential raw material that composes vision. A person with great ideas who doesn't grapple with the real issues, nitty-gritties and limitations of life as it is is not a visionary but a day-dreamer.

20/20 vision

What are you doing to develop and maintain your sense of vision? Read the following sets of statements and then tick whichever is more applicable to you.

I have lots of long-term plans ☐	**OR**	I take life a week (or a month) at a time ☐
I consult with others to develop my team's direction ☐	**OR**	My team's objectives are laid down by someone else ☐

I focus on how my team fits into the overall strategy of the church ☐	**OR**	My main concern is that my team does its job well ☐
I regularly allocate time in my diary to pray and plan – and stick to it ☐	**OR**	I aim to spend time praying and planning, but usually opt out at the last minute to deal with the demands of the moment ☐
I encourage my team to try new ways of doing things ☐	**OR**	I prefer to stick with doing things the way I know will work ☐
The development of my team as individuals is just as important to me as the work they do ☐	**OR**	My team exists primarily to get the job done ☐

If you ticked mainly boxes in the left-hand column, your sense of vision is healthy, though don't allow yourself to fall into a false sense of security. If you ticked mainly boxes in the right-hand column, you have some hard thinking to do. Short-sightedness can be corrected but you'll need to work at it!

What's your vision?

Take some time to consider your vision for the team you're currently involved in, or one you are planning to set up. Think big – be realistic but don't focus on the difficulties. Summarise it below:

_____

_____

_____

The willingness to delegate

Delegation is an essential skill for every successful team leader. It's the art of being able to allocate appropriate work and responsibilities to each of your team members. It's a skill that most of us think we've mastered. But the real evidence often points to a very different conclusion.

The reason why a team exists in the first place is that a particular objective can be achieved better through the complementary efforts of a number of people than alone. It therefore follows that the main task of the team leader is to plan, organise, motivate and oversee the work in hand, helping each member to make the most of their individual talents for the overall advantage of the team. It is *not* to do everything themselves.

A good example of delegation in the Bible is Moses. The burden of leading Israel was an enormous one which eventually took its toll on the great man, whose father-in-law suggested that he appoint a number of elders and divide up the tasks. To his credit, Moses took this advice to heart and delegated the leadership responsibility.

Effective delegation will mean:

✔ More work can be accomplished
✔ Team members become involved and develop 'ownership' of the vision

✔ Team members achieve more of their potential
✔ The team leader is left free to tackle those tasks which best suit their own skills

Delegation is not in itself a difficult skill to learn (and we deal with it specifically in Section 3). Yet it's an area in which many leaders struggle. They are used to being in charge, and don't find it easy to let things go out of their control. Theoretically committed to the *concept* of developing the gifts and skills of others, their *practice* is quite often another thing altogether!

It's the Lone Ranger!

Some leaders are actually nothing more than Lone Rangers in rather poor disguise. Don't bother looking for the mask and white steed, but watch out for a team of frustrated Tontos! While they collect around them people they casually refer to as 'my team', and hand out menial jobs, they are careful to avoid giving away any real responsibility and authority. Training their team and providing support and feedback isn't high on their agenda. They struggle with the pressure of work, constantly complaining about how much they have to do, and almost developing a martyr complex, but at the same time their 'team' is left twiddling its thumbs. Lone Rangers see themselves as star players surrounded by an incidental supporting cast. We probably all know at least one Lone Ranger who's utterly convinced that they're a team builder! How do you know that it's not you?

It makes sense that in order to delegate, we must first be utterly convinced of its value, and then take the bold step of doing it. The truth is that, if we're honest, most of us find delegation threatening, and so we rationalise our unwillingness to do so in various ways. Though our excuses often centre around the apparent inadequacies in our team members, in fact they are just a cover for our own reluctance to delegate.

Excuses. . . excuses. . .

Have you ever caught yourself saying any of the following?

'If you want a job done properly, do it yourself.'

A view based on the belief that you can do the job better than anyone else on your team. Of course the truth is this may be true! Your own competence may have been the very reason you were put in charge of the team in the first place. However, the choice is not between the quality of your work and that of another team member. It's between the benefits of spending your time on a single task and those of using it to motivate, train and develop an effective team. And, added to that, if you allow yourself to get bogged down in detail, you will eventually lose sight of the 'big picture', which means your team members will never develop (at least not until they get so frustrated with you that they leave and find a better team with a more flexible leader!).

'If I let go of the reins, the team will fall apart.'

We all have an inbuilt fear of losing control. But delegation is not abdication. It's not about dumping a task or responsibility on someone else less qualified to cope and then leaving them to sink or swim. Good delegation is a process of releasing control in a planned and gradual way as a team member's confidence and ability grow. It means giving them room to manoeuvre while you are still holding the reins. But delegation is not just about giving away responsibility. Responsibility without authority is demeaning. The willingness to delegate authority is the key to building commitment.

'It's quicker to do it myself than explain it to someone else.'

This is probably true, but it's not the point. If you don't take the time to teach someone else to do a task, you will still be doing the same job yourself in ten years' time. Delegation is about long-term investment. It may be that you actually prefer and enjoy doing something yourself, but the skills of your team members will never be developed unless you give them training and opportunity.

'I don't want to ask too much of them.'

This can be a genuine concern, especially if you lead a team of volunteers who already cope with many other demands, and you are employed full time by the church. For this reason, some leaders would prefer to burn themselves out rather than risk asking too much of others. However, research has shown that most people prefer working for good delegators – and no one should be on the team unless they're prepared to contribute. So make sure that team members feel able to say no – but never rob them of the opportunity to say yes!

'They just aren't capable of making the right decisions.'

Real delegation involves giving away real responsibility and authority. It's too easy to take the power back yourself when problems arise, rather than helping team members to reach the right decisions themselves. Delegation must include giving members the freedom to make their own mistakes (a very effective way of learning!) and then standing by them. If the thought of this approach sounds difficult, its rewards are much greater levels of commitment, ownership and team spirit.

'It's no good trusting them, they'll just let me down.'

Those who don't delegate often claim that it's because there's no one trustworthy to delegate to. But people only prove themselves trustworthy through being trusted. It's a real chicken and egg situation. And as leader you need to initiate that trust. If you're tempted to complain that worthy team members just aren't available, it might be worth reflecting on what you would have done with Jesus' disciples if they had been the material you had to work with!

If at first they don't succeed. . .

Jesus was a true master of the art of delegation. In Luke 9 he sent his twelve disciples out to preach the good news and heal the sick *in his name*. In other words, he was willing to take the bold step of placing his reputation and the accomplishment of his mission in the hands of those far less skilled and mature than he was. But the phrase 'in his name' refers to more than just reputation: it is a matter of authority. Jesus was taking the step of giving away his authority to others. By the end of the chapter, just as the critics no doubt had predicted, the disciples proved totally inadequate to the task of healing a boy with an evil spirit and entered instead into an open fight over who was the most promising team member. But rather than laying them off, Jesus stuck with them and even repeated the same exercise – this time with seventy-two candidates (Luke 10)!

Delegation will always be a risky and messy business. Mistakes will be made. Not everyone we delegate to will succeed in their task or prove worthy of the trust placed in them (Judas for instance). But Jesus' example shows that all of this never amounts to an excuse not to do it.

The use of power

The Church does not need brilliant personalities, but faithful servants of Jesus and the brethren.

Dietrich Bonhoeffer

If servanthood is the calling of every Christian, it should be modelled most clearly by the church's leaders. In the Gospels we read of James and John trying to use their position to get the best seats with Jesus in heaven. The other disciples felt suitably indignant, so Jesus got them together and outlined his philosophy:

You know that the rulers of the Gentiles lord it over them, and that their high officials exercise authority over them. Not so with you. Instead, whoever wants to become great among you must be your servant, and whoever wants to be first must be your slave. (Mt 20:25–27)

Jesus, in his words and example, turned the accepted contemporary concept of leading upside-down by introducing the most radical model of leadership the world has ever seen.

Power is dangerous. As Lord Acton commented, 'Power tends to corrupt and absolute power corrupts absolutely.' The pages of history are littered with the sad proof of his conclusion. But Jesus demonstrated that this process need not be inevitable. Servant leadership was his antidote to what would otherwise become the corruptive influence of power – the most dangerous commodity of leadership.

All leaders handle power, whether they're responsible for thousands or for a group of ten. The big question is how that power is used. Even for the Christian, there is the constant temptation to abuse it to manipulate others and to satisfy one's own ends. In leading your group it is important to be ever aware of the subtle influence of power.

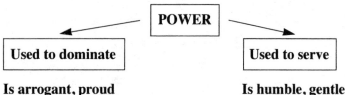

Used to dominate		Used to serve
Is arrogant, proud		Is humble, gentle
Seeks self-exaltation		Seeks to exalt others
Keeps control		Gives control away

The diagram above illustrates two totally different approaches to leadership. At one extreme is the person who leads because they need to be in charge. At the other is the person who sees leading as the best way in which they are able to serve others. There are as many ways of leading as there are leaders, but every leader will have the roots of their style in one of these two basic attitudes.

The dominating leader

The dominating leader is one who enjoys taking charge, making decisions and giving orders. And having gained control, he or she will use their power to keep a tight grip on it. However well disguised this attitude might be, because it's used to feed pride and arrogance, it will eventually lead to the breakdown and disintegration of relationships.

Arrogance has been described as the 'wrongness of those who think they are always right'. As a leader you may well have a proven ability to make good decisions on future matters. However, the down-side of that ability is that it can lead to a disregard of other people's viewpoints. However good a leader's ideas are, they will always be strengthened and sharpened by the advice, questioning and input of others.

Pride is an exaggerated sense of your own importance at the expense of others. Team members are viewed as support acts who exist for the leader's benefit. It's very important to remember that pride is not linked to any particular level of leadership; nor is it essentially the problem of a person whom others admire. Pride belongs to the person who, regardless of the position they occupy, looks down on others and assumes them to be inferior.

The truth is that those who dominate are often very insecure. They live with the fear that someone else may prove as successful as they are or, even worse, overtake and overshadow them. This lack of self-esteem shows itself in a **desire to exalt themselves** by devaluing others. But a leader who tries to look good at the expense of others will never keep a team (or at least the *same* team) long!

The dominating leader likes to **keep control** and is protective of power. He or she is reluctant to delegate any real authority, or share key insights and principles, for fear that, as an outcome, their dominion will suffer. For this reason, some church leaders reserve the right to have the final say on everything.

The servant leader

The servant leader, on the other hand, assumes leadership because they recognise it as the best way they can help and serve others. Their desire is not to be assertive or dominant, but rather to see others develop, progress, mature and achieve for themselves . . . and of course to get the job done. Therefore their people's best interests take priority over their own. Their service is not a 'means to an end', in which the aim is to move as quickly as possible to a place where others can serve them. They are servants for life.

Humility is the hidden badge of the servant leader. Where leadership in the church dominates rather than serves, it's completely alien to the whole tenor of the New Testament.

> *Do nothing out of selfish ambition or vain conceit, but in*
> *humility consider others better than yourselves. Each of*
> *you should look not only to his own interest, but also to*
> *the interests of others. Your attitude should be the same*
> *as that of Christ Jesus – who, being in very nature God,*
> *did not consider equality with God something to be*
> *grasped, but made himself nothing, taking the very nature*
> *of a servant, being made in human likeness.*
>
> (Phil 2:3–7)

Humility is not about being wimpish and self-debasing. The word originates from the Latin *humus*, meaning earth. It implies being down on ground level along with other people, as far as both attitudes and actions go.

The servant leader will **exalt others**. He or she will have high hopes for those in their team and will want them to develop and progress – even if it means they themselves are eclipsed in the process. It's only possible to do this from a position of security. Jesus had no qualms about washing his disciples' feet because he was secure in his position and his relationship with his Father. In the same way, if we are truly secure in our own relationship with God, we will understand that our position cannot be threatened or diminished by serving others.

The acquisition of greater power has no pull on a servant leader. They are not only willing to **give away the control** of power but positively seek ways of doing so. They understand that the selfish use of power will always enslave both those who use it and those who suffer it.

Service check

Tick the action which best describes your typical reaction in the given situation. Be sure to give an honest answer, rather than just the 'right' one!

1. You present a new idea to your team and someone immediately questions it. Do you:

(a) Begin formulating your defence even as they're speaking? ☐

(b) Concentrate on listening to them with an open mind and a relaxed attitude? ☐

(c) Assume they need reassuring as most people are a bit hesitant about changes? ☐

2. After a lot of convincing, your team has begun to work on a new approach you have suggested, with considerable success. A fellow leader remarks on the recent improvement. Do you:

(a) Give them the full details of your initial struggle – as a leader they'll appreciate it? ☐

(b) Explain exactly which members did what and give them all the credit? ☐

(c) Tell them about your initial struggle and the team's subsequent effort – credit where credit is due? ☐

3. A team member rings you to say that his mother has had a minor accident, but is in hospital. He would like to visit her that evening, which would mean breaking a speaking engagement with a local church youth group. Do you:

(a) Suggest a few people he could ring who might be able to stand in for him – though if no one is available you feel sure that the youth leader will understand? ☐

(b) Tell him not to worry about speaking and that if you can't find a replacement, you'll do it yourself? Ask if there's any other way you can help him? ☐

(c) Suggest a few people he could ask to replace him, adding that if he has no success he is to get back to you, and you will try to sort something out? ☐

4. The team you've been leading for three years has really developed. Some members have shown great leadership potential. Do you:

   (a) Begin to feel a bit jealous, threatened and insecure, and think about ways of improving your own leadership skills? ☐

   (b) Start thinking about whether this is the time for you to stand down or adopt a more 'hands off' role to make room for your team to develop further? ☐

   (c) Let your team know that if things continue to go well you are thinking about the possibility of increasing their responsibilities some time in the future? ☐

SCORE ANALYSIS

Mainly 'a's: You are either very new to team leadership, or else you, and consequently your whole team, have a big problem with your attitude.

Mainly 'b's: You are the sort of leader who could pull together a team to do almost anything – a servant through and through! You can take this praise because you're humble enough to handle it!

Mainly 'c's: Although you have some servant qualities, there is still a level of hesitation about going all the way. Be bold enough to take some risks, and put Jesus' example to the test. You'll be surprised by the results.

Who's left to lead?

If all the leaders are busy serving, you might wonder who's left to do the leading. It's vital to understand that Jesus was not promoting the view that leaders should abdicate their responsibility to lead in order to serve *instead*. Becoming a servant was not Jesus' alternative to being a strong leader. He spelt this out when he explained 'the one who rules' should be the one who serves. Servanthood is primarily a question of nature, not of function. It is the spirit in which we are called to express our leadership.

Trustworthiness

Leadership without mutual trust is a contradiction in terms. A leader has to trust their team in order to delegate, and each member has to trust their leader in order to accept their leadership. But trust is not so much an ingredient of servant leadership as its product. It is vital to build trust between a leader and a team because it's this that cements relationships, builds commitment and maintains unity in difficult times.

Trust is an initial act and an ongoing process. When Jesus saw Simon Peter and his brother Andrew fishing beside the Sea of Galilee, he said to them *'Come, follow me, and I will make you fishers of men'* (Mt 4:18). In leaving their nets and following Jesus, they made the choice to leave behind the security of their previous lifestyle and trust their future circumstances and situation to him. But an initial act is never enough to *sustain* trust, which can only develop in the context of an ongoing relationship. If, after following Jesus for a while, Peter and Simon had felt that the reality of the deal they got was not what they had initially signed up for, they would surely have packed their bags and gone home.

Over the course of three years, Jesus, the servant leader, slowly and carefully worked at building relationships of mutual trust with his disciples. And, in the final analysis, it was this that made them stick with him. Although they let him down, he never failed them. He always believed in them, and accepted the level of trust they were willing to give him, while at the same time encouraging them into a deeper relationship.

You cannot set up a team today and expect them to trust you totally tomorrow. Trust takes time to develop. You have to work at it.

What does trust involve?

The Oxford English Dictionary defines trust as 'firm belief in the reliability or truth or strength of a person or thing; a confident expectation'. In practice, this involves the following:

Making a choice   No one can ever force another person to trust them. Trust can only be given through free will. If trust isn't voluntary any superficial appearance of commitment will evaporate when the going gets tough.

Taking a risk   Trust is a risky business. You have to put faith in someone else's judgement with no cast iron guarantee. That's why it is generally easier to trust older leaders than younger ones. Even though a new leader's ideas may be just as good as an older one's (sometimes even better), it is track record which is the most crucial factor in winning trust.

Paying a price   Whenever you put your trust in someone else, you are making yourself vulnerable simply because you are giving away some control over your circumstances and future. Leaders need to appreciate the enormous cost of the trust people place in them.

How to become trustworthy

Those you lead will trust you to the degree that you have proved yourself to be trustworthy. So how do you develop a sense of trust from your team? What are the do's and don'ts? Here are a few ideas:

THINGS TO DO

☑ **Take the initiative:** Trust is mutual – it can only exist when both parties involved in a relationship are willing to give to each other. But it is always the leader's responsibility to set the pace. You must be the first to take the initiative. Leaders who trust their team are, in turn, trusted by them.

☑ **Affirm and encourage:** Make sure that you recognise your team's achievements. Be quick to give each member praise both publicly and privately. Here, once again, so many leaders fail. Though they are genuinely grateful for the contribution being made, they somehow rarely succeed in communicating their gratitude. Your team are not mind-readers. They can only appreciate your acceptance and recognition if you state it openly and unambiguously.

☑ **'Walk the talk':** Your actions must endorse your words. One of the most common reasons people don't trust leaders is because they recognise a credibility gap between their words and actions. In true leaders, there is no gap between what they say and how they live their lives.

☑ **Be reliable:** Don't let people down. Prove your trustworthiness through the reliable and conscientious way in which you undertake your responsibilities. Once you have accepted a task, no matter how difficult, make sure that it is done to the best of your ability and on time. If you feel you are being forced to work under too much pressure, learn how to take on fewer responsibilities in the first place. Don't dump or neglect them once you have committed yourself.

☑ **Keep promises**: This must be one of your golden rules. Don't be tempted to think that it doesn't apply to you because the issue in question is only small, or because it will be of such great cost or inconvenience to you. Never make excuses for yourself in this area. Your yes must be yes and your no, no. If your team don't feel able to trust you with small things, they will be unable to put their faith in you when it comes to more important matters.

☑ **Be honest:** Dishonesty corrodes trust. You cannot trust someone unless you are sure they are being honest and open with you. Avoid reshaping or editing the truth for a particular audience: although you cannot be accused of lying, you will discover that those you lead slowly come to the point where they take everything you say with a pinch of salt.

☑ **Be loyal:** Loyalty means that you can be relied on to be there, no matter what the cost or risk to yourself. It means that you can never be accused of being simply a 'fair-weather friend'. People need to know that you will not abandon them, even in times of trouble.

☑ **Be accountable:** Leaders often make the fatal mistake of thinking that their team expects them to be infallible. This is not true! When mistakes are made, as they are bound to be made by any leader, what people look for is not denial, cover-up and excuses, but the honesty to recognise what has happened, and the courage to apologise and look for new ways forward. People invest too much in their leaders to accept feeling deceived by them. Such accountability will only ever serve to strengthen trust.

THINGS NOT TO DO

☒ **Don't expect too much too soon:** Remember that trust is a progressive thing which has to be built between team and leader slowly. Your aim is not to push your team to the limit by devising the toughest test you can in order to see whether or not they can be trusted. Though they have already made an initial commitment to you, it requires time and opportunity for both you and them to build on it.

☒ **Don't criticise:** When people fail, many leaders make the mistake of taking one of two ill-chosen ways of dealing with the situation. Either they ignore the situation altogether, a reaction motivated by their fear of confrontation, or they over-react to it, heaping out criticism and blame, which serves only to knock confidence further. Instead of falling into the trap of either of these negative responses, use the situation positively by making time to sit down and help team members understand where and how they can improve on their contribution. Your encouragement and practical advice will help to equip them for future success.

☒ **Don't be inconsistent:** It is very difficult for those you lead to trust you if they cannot be sure how you will react in any particular situation. You should aim to be consistent in your behaviour and responses, however you feel!

☒ **Don't break confidences:** The discovery that something shared in confidence is now common knowledge will guarantee the instant destruction of trust. Never pass on information that you have received in confidence unless you first seek and receive permission from the confidant.

☒ **Don't show favouritism:** If you want to maintain the trust of your team, you must avoid showing favouritism or discrimination of any sort. It is your task to act even-handedly in all matters. Once some of your team believe they are being discriminated against, not only will their own trust in you disappear, they will also begin to destroy it within others.

☒ **Don't complain:** Remember, nobody forced you to become a leader! Your team might complain when things are not going the way they want them to, but you must not give in to the same temptation. Don't be negative and never try to blackmail people by threatening to give up. Nothing you could do or say will have a more unsettling effect on those you lead, and nothing you can do or say will ever remove the memory of your words or the impact they have had, even when things get better.

Accountability

Accountability is perhaps the most demanding quality any leader is required to exhibit. To be accountable is to hold yourself genuinely answerable to others for your actions, decisions, performance and results. While few of us struggle with the privileges and power that come with the leadership package, many are less enthusiastic about the restraints that accountability imposes on them. In fact, for many leaders for whom the natural inclination is to 'get on with the job', the idea of having to listen to the opinions and views of others regarding how they are doing is a very difficult medicine to have to swallow.

But accountability is the price of power, and should be equal to it. However small or large the team or church you are responsible for is, the principle is the same. The degree of power and trust invested in you is equal to the level of your accountability.

Jesus modelled accountability. He never used his position or authority to please himself. He did only those things which his Father told him to, even in the most pressurised situations. Sadly, illustrations of the lack of accountability are all too frequent in today's public arena. Our newspapers are filled with stories of those who abuse the privilege of power and position, and become a law unto themselves. Tragically, the same problem is sometimes all too evident within the church.

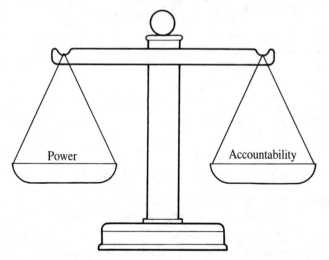

There are three important questions to consider regarding accountability. **Why** should leaders be accountable? **For what** should leaders be accountable? And **to whom** should leaders be accountable?

True or false?

Read each of the following statements. Tick whether you think they are true or false, then read on . . .

	TRUE	FALSE
1. My ultimate accountability only goes as far as the responsibilities people have trusted me with.	☐	☐
2. Accountability is a safeguard against the misuse of power.	☐	☐
3. The levels of responsibility I am trusted with will increase as I prove that I am accountable.	☐	☐
4. Accountability helps produce endurance.	☐	☐
5. My team members are more accountable to me than I am to them.	☐	☐

6. As a leader, I am accountable to God,
   rather than to others. ☐ ☐
7. Accountability restricts my freedom and
   self-fulfilment. ☐ ☐
8. If my team members fail in their task,
   I must shoulder the responsibility before
   others in the church. ☐ ☐

WHY should leaders be accountable?

Because it provides a *safeguard*. Accountability acts as a necessary and healthy guard against the misuse of power. If we have to give an account of our actions, we think twice before using our position to serve our own selfish ends. Power has a tendency to corrupt and therefore the absence of accountability paves the way for it to slide towards dictatorship. Evidence of this is seen both within the church and outside it. Even under extreme pressure, Jesus refused to act in a selfish manner. In the Garden of Gethsemane, knowing that betrayal, arrest and crucifixion awaited him, he still prayed, *'Father, if you are willing, take this cup from me; yet not my will, but yours be done'* (Lk 22:42). He understood that he was accountable to his Father and chose not to opt out of that responsibility.

Because it provides a *challenge*. Accountability helps to create perseverance in a leader. It will help sustain them when the going gets tough and the pressure is mounting. At times, we all feel like opting out of commitments made in a more enthusiastic moment. Knowing that we have to report back can spur us on to do our best even in difficult circumstances.

Because it provides a *framework*. It is only with the protection created by genuine accountability that any leader can operate with confidence and freedom. Jesus made it clear on several occasions that, at all times, he operated within the mandate given him by his Father: *'For I have come down from heaven, not to do* *my will but to do the will of him who sent me'* (Jn 6:38). To be responsible to others provides a supportive framework within which a leader can enjoy working in the knowledge that they are doing what is required of them. As in many other areas of life, freedom and fulfilment are not the result of throwing off restrictions, but of accepting their legitimacy and welcoming the framework they create.

FOR WHAT are leaders accountable?

For their talents and opportunities. In the parable of the talents (Mt. 25:14–30), Jesus makes two very clear points about our accountability for the gifts and opportunities we are given. First of all, we are nothing more than stewards. Our talents do not originate with us. They are entrusted to us by God, who therefore holds us accountable for them. We are ultimately responsible to him for the way we use them. Secondly, the parable illustrates that responsibility is just like trust: it increases only as we prove ourselves capable of handling it. We can have a tendency to look at other leaders and ask why they have been given more opportunity or responsibility than us. But as John Perry says in his book *Christian Leadership*, 'many a prominent Christian leader today laid strong foundations in the past by the way they handled smaller responsibilities which they tackled in comparative obscurity'. *'You have been faithful with a few things,'* the master said to the servants who invested their talents well. *'I will put you in charge of many things.'*

For those they lead. One of the most sobering aspects of the role of a leader is simply this: when people trust their leader, they are in effect giving up control of some aspect of their future. They are making themselves vulnerable. This means that a leader is answerable for any failure to care for them or to put their interests at the top of his or her agenda. Hebrews 13:17 states *'Obey your leaders and submit to their authority,'* but then quickly adds, *'They keep watch over you as those who must give an account.'*

When we delegate jobs to our team, we must also delegate the responsibility that goes with them. But they are still responsible back to us, and therefore we must retain accountability for them before others if things go wrong. A mark of a good leader is the willingness to carry the can when things fall apart.

TO WHOM are leaders accountable?

To God. Ultimately, as Jesus illustrated by his example and teaching, every leader is accountable to God. In fact, it is clear from the parable of the talents that this is the case regardless of whether or not they acknowledge it. The Bible is clear that every secular leader, as well as every church leader, will eventually find themselves answerable to God for the way they have used and invested their gifts.

To other leaders. No leader should work alone. Every leader should have a team of other leaders to whom they are or have made themselves accountable. If this is not the case, the claim that we are under 'God's authority' becomes in effect a kind of spiritual shorthand for, 'I am accountable to no one and do as I please.' It's often pointed out that religious sects are marked by the lack of external accountability of their leadership. But to be accountable to others does not mean gathering around you a group of 'yes men' who will automatically back whatever you choose to do. You will be strongest when those you are answerable to are also people of strength, whom you trust and respect, and to whom you will genuinely submit.

Depending on your denomination or stream, you may have formal accountability to those beyond your local church. Where this relationship is based on commitment and mutual trust, it can be very valuable. But if the relationship consists of formality alone it will mean very little. However formal accountability might work out in practice, it should not detract from the importance of being accountable to those who know and work with you in the local setting.

To those they lead. Less publicised, but equally true, is the fact that leaders must be accountable to those they lead. Frequently keen for their team to be accountable to them, leaders are not always so quick to recognise that accountability is 'a two-way street'. Every leader should be answerable to those who have trusted them and therefore have, in effect, delegated to them the power and authority of leadership.

Practical accountability

In what practical ways do you make yourself accountable to:

Other leaders?   Those you lead?

_____   _____

_____   _____

_____   _____

_____   _____

_____   _____

As you have by now guessed, the answers to statements 1, 5, 6 and 7 are FALSE; 2, 3, 4 and 8 are TRUE.

SECTION 3

Skills of Team Leadership

*'Acquiring skill is learning to bring
behaviour into line with your intentions.'*
John Adair

Communicating and motivating

*The more seasoned communicator understands
from experience that if the heart and imagination
and feelings are not moved, reason probably will
not persuade.*
                                                    Leighton Ford

To have a great vision for your team is one thing; to communicate that vision to them and motivate them to achieve is another.

Most of us have been on the receiving end of a leader's desperate pleas for willing volunteers for essential tasks. Perhaps we have even resorted to using the same kind of 'last ditch' arm-twisting tactics ourselves. Desperate need can lead to desperate measures. Somehow, we instinctively know that emotional pressure and pointed sermons are not the best way to produce enthusiastic teams. But, if that's not the way to do it – what is?

The key to building a committed team lies first in understanding that *people are primarily motivated by people*, not concepts, ideas and projects. It is, therefore, your character, your attitude, and the way you communicate that will determine whether others will want to 'sign up' and get involved. Do you need to find a few more people for your youth leadership team or increase the commitment of your worship group? Do you want to put together a team to plant a new church, or to clean the loos at your annual camp? Whatever the task, the question of whether you get an enthusiastic response from others lies in your own hands!

What's getting across?

An effective team leader must also be an effective communicator. As Bernard Baruch put it, 'The ability to express an idea is well nigh as important as the idea itself.' In other words, it's not just what you say, but the way that you say it. Jesus, the most remarkable communicator the world has ever known, showed a striking ability to choose his words to suit the particular occasion and audience. He knew how to connect with an excited crowd or a worried individual, a casual contact or a desperate inquirer.

Communication is an art, not a science. Sciences are rigid. Thus $2 + 2 = 4$, not $4\frac{1}{2}$ or 4 and a little bit. But arts are different. Although there are certain fundamental principles, there is lots of room for innovation, interpretation and style. There is more to being a great musician than just the ability to play the right notes, for example. Nevertheless, understanding the ground rules is an essential place to start.

There are three basic groups of skills which you use every time you communicate:

VERBAL   These skills cover the words you use, the content of your message; what you actually say.

VOCAL   The vocal skills involve the way you speak – for instance, the tone and inflection of your voice.

VISUAL   These skills relate to how your face and body communicate – for instance, how you sit or stand, the way you move, and your expressions.

Your communication is most effective when the verbal, vocal and visual aspects of your message are all working together in harmony. We have tended to give the vast majority of our attention to the *content* of our message, because this has been viewed as the most important. But the problem is that if our vocal and visual skills are poor, our message will lack *credibility* – one of the key ingredients of effective communication.

All the research and our personal experience point us to the same conclusion. When the verbal, vocal and visual elements are inconsistent, it is the verbal message which gets lost. For instance, the statement 'I'm so excited about the new evangelism team we are setting up' is completely undermined by the person who speaks in a halting monotone while shuffling nervously from foot to foot, staring at the floor. Those listening will unfortunately end up with a message that actually says, 'I'm bored and embarrassed by the new evangelism team!'

Seeing and believing

Vocal and visual skills have traditionally been something of a blind spot for many church leaders. We can spend hours working on *what* we want to say while hardly giving a second thought to *how* we communicate our message. To consider what we might *look* like can seem positively 'unspiritual'! And yet, at the same time, many of us know that we have been brought up on a diet of extremely sound sermons which left us feeling uninspired and bored, and even guilty for feeling that way.

The problem is not so much with the content as with the communicator. Have you ever wondered why so many experts are boring? They know almost everything there is to know about their particular discipline, and obviously find it extremely interesting. But as soon as they start talking about it, they have the effect of putting everyone to sleep more effectively than sleeping tablets. Why? Because their wealth of expertise stops short of the ability to communicate.

If the gospel is the most exciting message in the world, why do so many people describe the church as boring? Why do sermons have such a bad reputation? Perhaps it's because we have filled our pulpits with those with the most knowledge, regardless of their ability to communicate. The world will never be won to Christ by theological accuracy alone, but by people who have learned to communicate the reality of the Christian message in a way that others can understand. A meal may be highly nutritious, but whether it is eaten or not is often far more dependent on the question of how it is presented. Just ask a chef, or a mother.

If you want to assess how well you communicate, here are three suggestions:

- Ask a good friend to assess you
- Listen to yourself on tape
- Watch yourself on video – get someone to record you on a camcorder

In each instance, note your strong points as well as your weak spots. Obviously the feed-back from a friend is the most objective and therefore probably the most valuable. In the short term, it takes great courage to do this, but in the long term you will find it enormously beneficial. Remember, communication is not about trying to 'create the right image', but about making sure that what people hear corresponds with what you were trying to say.

More than words

Skilful communication is a key asset for any leader. But in the long term it's your life which will endorse your words and eventually determine how seriously people listen to you. Credibility is about *lifestyle*.

Caught not taught

Your personal attitude is highly infectious and will be communicated, like it or not, in all sorts of subtle and subconscious ways. If you are genuinely excited about your team, others will catch your attitude. If you are not, the same will be true. *Enthusiasm* in a team leader is a prerequisite for the development of an enthusiastic team. Are you totally convinced about your team, its purpose and task? Check up on yourself by ticking which of the following statements apply to you:

I don't particularly enjoy talking about my team, but will if pushed. ☐	**OR**	I talk about my team all the time to anyone who will listen. ☐
I don't like to keep talking about my vision because I might bore people. ☐	**OR**	People close to me could describe my vision, they've heard it so often. ☐
I find it hard to sum up what my team is trying to achieve. ☐	**OR**	I could sum up my team's purpose in one sentence. ☐
If I can't get a team together for this project I might try something else. ☐	**OR**	If I can't get a team together for this project I'll do it myself! ☐

RESULT: If you've ticked the statements in the right-hand column, you might run the risk of occasionally boring a few close friends, but you've every chance of inspiring a team! If you've ticked those in the left-hand column, then you need to re-evaluate what you are doing and why. Remember, enthusiasm and apathy are both infectious.

What motivates

Others might appreciate, even admire, the concept behind your team, they might agree that it will play an essential role in the life of the church, they may even be convinced of its success – but none of that will of itself motivate them to join up, or decide to stay on board.

Aristotle taught that effective communication consisted of combining:

logos   (the essence of the **message**),
ethos   (the **credibility** of the messenger) and
pathos (the **appeal to the inner motives** of the hearer).

God made us with certain basic 'inner' or psychological needs, which we are all motivated to satisfy. They centre around our need for *love*, *security* and *significance*. If membership of your team provides a sense of belonging, purpose, meaning and value, then you are much more likely to win, and keep, their support.

Check your motivation potential: **YES**   **NO**

LOVE	Do you genuinely *care* about the people you work with – rather than seeing them as tools to achieve your team objectives?	☐	☐
SECURITY	Will membership of your team create a real *sense of belonging*? Will relationships be important? Will it be fun?	☐	☐
SIGNIFICANCE	Will involvement in your team give people an opportunity to do what is important to them? Will they feel they are playing a *worthwhile* part in a task that really matters? Will it be *challenging* and give scope for real *accomplishment*?	☐	☐

These are some of the questions people will be asking, at least subconsciously, as you explain your new idea for a social action team that you are sure will transform local community life. It's your job not only to recognise this but to ensure your vision accommodates it.

Choosing your team

The art of choosing the right members for a team is crucial to its success. Management experts suggest three factors you should look for:

- Technical or professional competence
- Ability to work as a team member
- Desirable personal attributes

Modern business management theory stresses the paramount importance of always choosing qualified personnel:

Human resources are the most critical part of any organisation's success. Good people help to ensure profitability, growth and long-term survival. You simply cannot survive without qualified people.

R. Maddux

All of this makes good sense, but the apostle Paul had a very important rider to add to our thinking on the issue:

Think of what you were when you were called. Not many of you were wise by human standards; not many were influential; not many were of noble birth. But God chose the foolish things of the world to shame the wise; God chose the weak things of the world to shame the strong.

(1 Cor 1:26–27)

To many management consultants, Paul's perspective might sound rather worrying. But the church is, without doubt, the most successful organisation ever in terms of its growth and, of course, its long-term survival. And it all began with a bunch of unqualified fishermen and a slightly dodgy tax collector! Jesus obviously knew what it took to make a team work, but did not restrict himself to those with proven ability. He had the ability to spot the potential in people and was willing to take calculated risks in order to develop them.

X-ray vision

When Jesus looked at people he saw what they could be, he looked for their undiscovered skills and abilities, not just their existing areas of competence (or incompetence!). When Andrew brought his brother Simon to Jesus, Jesus said, *'You are Simon son of John. You will be called Cephas'* (which, when translated, is Peter or 'Rocky'). Those who knew Simon, knew that he could be unreliable and impetuous and must have at least questioned Jesus' wisdom. Peter was more 'wobbly' than rock-like! Yet, as a result of Jesus' trust and training, Simon did eventually become Peter, the strong, dependable and wise founder member and leader of the church.

A sculptor has the vision to get excited about what most of us would perceive as an ugly old lump of wood. Their excitement is to do with their ability to see beyond the obvious. In fact, many sculptors describe their work not in terms of creating a form but rather as 'setting free' what already exists. When they have finished chipping away, what they could always see finally becomes apparent to all.

In this context, vision could be described as *'the ability to see beneath the surface of people's lives'*. Most of us can spot the obvious in people, especially their faults, but a visionary looks deeper and focuses on potential. Choosing team members on this basis will certainly involve taking risks with people, and not everyone will prove a diamond in the making, but sometimes the most dubious raw material can yield surprising results if we are prepared to work hard and be patient.

Modern business theory is geared towards playing safe. That's what makes Jesus' approach so different. In stark contrast to the majority of contemporary organisations and companies, which place high value on proven track record and lack the flexibility to take risks, local churches should be prepared to recognise and invest in latent potential.

Three ingredients

In the light of all this, what should our approach be towards the three qualities mentioned at the beginning of this chapter?

- **Technical or professional competence**

  It's essential that the members of your team either have some actual or potential skill in the relevant area – but look beyond the obvious. For instance, if you're putting together a finance team it might be tempting to confine your approaches to those involved day to day in the world of banking and not to look beyond those limits (except in desperation!). But it may well be that those involved in finance all week have enough of sorting out money without doing it in their spare time as well. They might come alive through the challenge of getting involved in something completely different. The safe option is rarely the most imaginative one.

  But remember, the members of your team should have *some* actual or potential skills. A tone deaf singer, no matter how enthusiastic, is hardly an asset to the worship group! It is equally true that enthusiasm and limited experience are more useful to the team than excellence in someone who thinks that they have nothing to learn. People are rarely fully aware of their talents, especially if they have never had the opportunity to test them. So don't be put off by any initial hesitancy due to lack of confidence. You might need to have more belief in a team member's latent talents than they do.

- **Ability to work as a team member**
  Skills and competence alone will not make a team work. If a gifted individual refuses to work as part of a team, and has the sort of 'Lone Ranger' attitude we looked at in Section 2 of this book, then their value to your team will be limited. Team members should be able to work alongside other people, or at least be willing to learn. The ability to be flexible and to listen to other people always helps, as does a sense of humour. Individuals like this will provide a good foundation on which to build.

- **Desirable personal attributes**
  Your task is not just to build and maintain a team. Every team leader is also charged with the duty to develop and shape the character of individual team members. But once again, don't expect perfection overnight. Jesus accepted people as they were and took it from there. Your task is to have the insight, patience and commitment to others to do the same.

The bigger picture

Be sensitive to the overall chemistry of your team. It's tempting to opt for people with whom you naturally click because, in fact, they are just like you! This is damaging, if not fatal, in the longer term. Your team will be strongest if it contains a broad spectrum of personalities who are able to complement each other, rather than simply clones of yourself. Aim for *balance*. You need a mix of personality and temperament – not all introverts or extroverts. You need people with ideas, and people able to transform those ideas into reality. You need radicals and conservatives, those who see the opportunities and openings, and those who see the pitfalls and ask the tough questions. A leader with team members who always see things in the same way as they do, and agree with everything they say, reaps the counsel of mediocrity.

Checklist

The following checklist will help you in considering an individual's suitability for your team.

		YES	NO
1.	Does this person have the actual or potential skill for the task?	☐	☐
2.	Is he or she motivated to seek excellence?	☐	☐
3.	Is he or she flexible enough to work with others?	☐	☐
4.	Will they complement the rest of the team?	☐	☐
5.	Have they a sense of humour and a tolerance of others?	☐	☐
6.	Are they be willing to serve in any capacity that might be required?	☐	☐
7.	Will they develop a sense of *group* responsibility?	☐	☐
8.	Do they have a realistic appreciation of their own strengths and weaknesses?	☐	☐
9.	Do they have the respect of those who know them?	☐	☐
10.	Would the team help them develop their gifts and abilities?	☐	☐

A majority of positive answers points to a useful new member of your team. More than a couple of negatives will mean that your work as team leader will be that much more challenging. If you're not sure, talk in confidence to another leader for a second opinion. But remember, people will never develop their potential unless someone is willing to take a risk with them.

Goals and objectives

Goals and objectives are the practical way in which your vision will be translated into reality. The effective team leader must take time to identify and define them.

A road to nowhere?

Before you set out on any journey you need to know three things:

1. Where you want to go to (*destination*)
2. Where you are at the moment (*starting point*)
3. How you are going to get there (*route*)

Only when you are fully aware of both your destination and your starting point can you work out your route. To set off for a destination without having researched your route is foolish and potentially disastrous. So how do we apply the lesson of the roads to the task of effective teamwork?

Setting goals

Terminology can sometimes be very confusing. The terms used in this chapter are defined as follows:

Goal = *destination*. This is the end to which all your team efforts are directed.

Objectives = *route*.   These are the shorter steps you need to take in order to reach your destination.

It is always your **goal** which needs to be settled first. You might aim to reach it one, three, or more years ahead. But regardless of the time-frame you choose to set yourself, it is the exact nature of this goal which you need to define. How will you know when you get there? Unless you are clear about where you are heading, you can't hope to direct others, and will waste a great deal of time going round in circles yourself.

Once you've defined your goal, it's essential to break it down into a number of smaller **objectives**, or steps, by which you will achieve it and by which you will be able to monitor your progress. They must be set firmly, but at the same time need to be flexible in the sense that, just as a closed road might force you to change your route, so circumstances may necessitate a changed approach in order that you make it to your destination.

One step at a time

However far ahead you've set your sights, the only way to get there is one step at a time.

If, for example, my goal is to build a shed, I might break that task down into five smaller objectives:

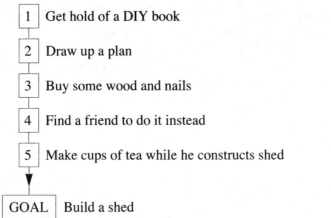

1 Get hold of a DIY book

2 Draw up a plan

3 Buy some wood and nails

4 Find a friend to do it instead

5 Make cups of tea while he constructs shed

GOAL Build a shed

Depending on the nature of your team's task, you should break it down into manageable, smaller objectives. It's important to give your most detailed thought to crossing the ground immediately ahead of you, since this is what you can see most clearly. But all objectives, in order to work, must have some specific built-in components.

WHAT? Be *specific* about your objectives. They should be big enough to present *a challenge*, but also *realistic* enough to attain. If they are set too high or low, they will fail to inspire much enthusiasm.

HOW? You need to decide how each objective is to be achieved and what resources are needed to attain the desired result. This means that you will also need to decide *who* will be responsible for the particular tasks involved.

WHEN? Finally, you need a *measurable* time period during which each of your objectives should be completed – a realistic *deadline*. 'As soon as possible' results in fuzziness, which makes any progress difficult to evaluate.

Team ownership

In setting your goal, and especially your objectives, it's vital to involve your team. This will obviously involve planning time together to do this. Talk openly and honestly about the strategy. Ask for their help, advice and ideas and listen to what they say. If goals and objectives are discussed and understood by your team, a sense of 'ownership' will develop, and they will feel far more responsible for the outcome. Goals and objectives that are imposed on any team without consultation will rarely, if ever, be owned by them.

Individual goals

Once your objectives are settled, it is time to allocate individual tasks. Each member of your team needs clear *personal* objectives which they regard as their responsibility to see achieved. These should always be worked through and agreed with the individual concerned, and objectives should be geared towards their personal strengths and skills. Just like team objectives, these personal objectives should also be specific and time-framed, as well as realistic and challenging. The process of how to allocate tasks to individual team members is discussed in Section 4, 'Training for Success'.

If you miss . . .

There is little point in setting objectives unless you take time subsequently to reflect on and review how you're doing. The team should meet regularly to assess their progress. If objectives have not been achieved, you should ask the following questions:

- What went wrong?
- Why?
- What problems were ignored or underestimated?
- Were the reasons for failure inside or outside the team's control?
- How can this problem be overcome?
- Could the problems have been foreseen?
- How can the team work to revise the objectives?

Remember that objectives are just a means to an end; not the end itself. They are not set in concrete, and may need adjusting as you review your progress. It is important never to lose sight of your goal, but, just as on any journey, remember that there are a number of different routes to get somewhere. To go a slower route might be more sensible and actually better for the development of your team.

Mapping the route

Depending on the nature of your team, you may have just one goal or you might have several. Whatever the case, your goals and objectives should always be written down. In Section 2 we gave some thought to your vision for your team. Now try defining that vision as a specific goal, or series of goals. Then work with your team on breaking them down into measurable, manageable and timed objectives.

Our goal is: _____

_____

Some objectives to reach it are:

1. _____

2. _____

3. _____

4. _____

5. _____

If you've defined your objectives well, you should be able to tick all the following.

Objective no.	1	2	3	4	5
SPECIFIC	☐	☐	☐	☐	☐
ATTAINABLE	☐	☐	☐	☐	☐
MEASURABLE	☐	☐	☐	☐	☐
CHALLENGING	☐	☐	☐	☐	☐
TIMED	☐	☐	☐	☐	☐

Delegation

Earlier, we looked at *why* we should delegate. Now, we come to the vital issue of *how* to do it.

Delegation is not about off-loading mundane and unwanted tasks onto team members. That's just dumping! It's the process by which a leader provides them with opportunities to develop new skills, handle responsibility, gain confidence and so achieve success. (Section 4, 'Training for Success', considers your team's needs in more detail.)

Successful delegation is the result of a leader taking a number of essential steps:

D eciding what to delegate
E lecting who to delegate to
L isting what's involved
E xplaining the task
G iving adequate training
A llowing freedom to work
T elling others about the delegation
E valuating performance

Deciding what to delegate

Which of the day-to-day responsibilities you carry could be handled by others? If you delegated a significant proportion of these you would have more time to plan ahead and so lead your team more effectively. Begin by making a list of the tasks you could delegate. And think radically! Here is a list to help stimulate your thoughts:

- **Tasks that you're good at:** These are most likely things you enjoy doing but which other people could be trained to do equally well. Why not share your skill with someone else?
- **Tasks that you're bad at:** There will certainly be some things your team members can do better than you. Be a talent spotter and then let them get on with it.
- **Work which will provide experience:** Your team members will enjoy the challenge of learning new skills and increasing their experience, so give them the chance.
- **Opportunities to reinforce talents:** Build on the strengths of your team members, rather than their weaknesses. If they have real talent, give them the freedom to develop it as best they can.
- **Routine decisions:** Increase your team's responsibility by delegating decisions which don't necessarily require your input.

Electing who to delegate to

It's essential that you consider carefully exactly who will be suitable to take on each responsibility. Ask the following questions:

- Who has the talent and potential skill to suit the task?
- Who has the time and enthusiasm to learn?
- Who would find the work challenging?
- Who would benefit the most from doing it?

If you jump in without thinking, you are likely to end up giving the wrong jobs to the wrong people. It might not be wise, for instance, to ask your talented and enthusiastic drummer to organise the entertainment for the over-60s' afternoon tea!

Listing what's involved

Without a clear understanding of specific tasks and responsibilities, any attempt to delegate is bound to backfire. Lack of planning will result in a confused brief.

- What is the task or responsibility and what results are required?
- What skills and abilities will be needed?
- How much time is it likely to take?
- By when does it need to be done?

Explaining the task

Describe the task as fully as possible face to face with your team member. Once a delegation has been agreed in theory, you should draw up a draft description of the job and invite their feedback. This brief should always be *written*. Make sure it is very practical – assume nothing. You can then discuss and agree it together. This will minimise confusion and serve as a blueprint, should any problem occur.

It's also important to let your team member know the amount of authority and responsibility that you are delegating. This will depend upon the nature of the task and your confidence in the person to whom you delegate. This is also a good opportunity to encourage them, and to make sure that they know that their involvement is valued.

Giving adequate training

This principle is the forgotten secret at the heart of all delegation. To delegate is not a quick way of finding out whether or not a team member is up to a task – a case of whether they will sink or swim. What training or special help do you need to give them to ensure their success? Be sure you provide it by making yourself available to them.

Allowing freedom to work

Monitor progress, but don't interfere. Having given away responsibility, don't keep sticking your nose in. You will know from your own experience that there's nothing worse than being given a job and then having someone constantly interfering and changing the decisions you make. This only succeeds in demotivating, breeding resentment and diminishing trust. Your task is to learn to cope with the difficult balance between over- and under-caring by being available to those to whom you delegate, remembering that once you've delegated a task you must let your team member use their initiative as to exactly how it might be achieved.

Telling others about the delegation

Once you have delegated a task (especially if it's one you've done for a long time), make sure that other people on your team, anyone else who will be directly affected, and the rest of your church are informed of the change. In this way, you give your authority publicly to the person to whom you've delegated. This in itself will give them confidence, help them to take their task seriously, and keep the lines of communication open.

As team leader, you must still be prepared to carry the can publicly if things go wrong. Being willing to do this is essential for team loyalty – the reasons for any failure should be discussed privately not publicly.

Evaluating performance

Without regular assessment, your team members won't know whether they are doing a good, bad or indifferent job. Nobody enjoys working in a vacuum. Monitor each person's performance and *schedule regular feedback sessions*. These should take place quite frequently at first (eg, once a week or fortnight) and become less frequent as your team member's confidence grows. Such meetings provide an opportunity for honest, positive comments on both successes and failures. If something goes wrong, rather than reacting in the heat of the moment, this feedback session provides the context to discuss together the reasons why and the corrective action required.

Following this process means that you have a chance to reflect on the situation and moderate your thoughts before 'speaking your mind'! Added to this, if, when you meet, you allow your team member to go through a list of any difficulties they have perceived first, you may often find that the problem concerned was beyond their control, and that your proposed comments would therefore have been uncalled for and unhelpful!

Remember that delegation is not a one-off act. It is a process. As a team member's confidence increases, your involvement should slowly diminish. Regular assessment will keep things on track. Never take a job back unless it is absolutely essential.

In summary, make sure that your team members are:

- Given any training they need
- Motivated by new challenges as their skills develop
- Supported whenever they need it
- Given opportunities to do what's important to them
- Encouraged to reach their potential
- Praised both privately and publicly for good work done.

Initially, delegation is *always* time consuming. But if proper briefing, training and feedback are given at this stage, you will find that your investment pays long-term dividends.

List three tasks you could delegate, and commit yourself to taking some positive action to do it!

To be delegated . . .

THE TASK	1 _____	2 _____	3 _____
The reason	_____	_____	_____
Who to	_____	_____	_____
Training needs	_____	_____	_____
The deadline	_____	_____	_____

Making decisions

'Why didn't they ask me first?'

'I could have told them it wouldn't work!'

'Typical! He makes yet another stupid decision and then expects me to sort it all out for him!'

How many times have you heard comments like these? Nothing demotivates people more and generates hostility faster than the frustration of not being consulted, included or involved in decisions that affect them, their work, and their vision.

Many routine decisions are made simply to keep your team's wheels in motion. But others are more significant and will therefore have a far greater effect. Whenever leadership decisions will have an impact on other people, it's vital that you tackle them wisely.

A fine example

In Acts 6, a dispute arises in the Jerusalem church when a certain group feels that its widows are not receiving the quality of pastoral care they are entitled to from the apostles. As a result, the apostles meet to talk the situation over, and choose to make seven new appointments to the leadership team. The job of these new recruits is to do the practical work for which the apostles' timetable no longer allows. In other words, a problem is recognised, the facts are assessed, those with a complaint are heard, a clear decision is made, the church is informed and action is taken in the form of appointing a group of second-tier leaders who are answerable to the apostles.

Decisive stages

The appointment of these seven is a very clear example of how to make a good leadership decision. There are basically five stages, which are just as applicable today as in first-century Palestine. Though sticking to these will not guarantee you get it right all the time, they will significantly increase your success rate.

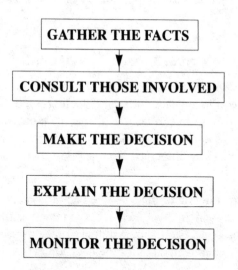

GATHER THE FACTS

↓

CONSULT THOSE INVOLVED

↓

MAKE THE DECISION

↓

EXPLAIN THE DECISION

↓

MONITOR THE DECISION

Pause for thought

Think of a recent important leadership decision that you have been involved in, or even better still, one that you know has to be made soon.

As you read through the five steps of decision making below, apply them to your real-life situation.

GATHER THE FACTS

Avoid making important decisions on the spur of the moment or solely on the basis of your initial feelings. Give yourself time to assess all the relevant information. Always ask yourself:

- What facts do I need to know before I can make this decision? Never make an important decision until you are in possession of all the relevant information – give yourself time to collect it.
- What is the deadline for this decision? Don't rush into making a decision today if you actually have more time. Write down the issues involved in order to clarify what has to be decided, as well as the results you are hoping to achieve.

CONSULT THOSE INVOLVED

The word 'consult' means 'to seek information or advice from, and to take into consideration the feelings and interests of, others'. It does not mean asking for people's blessing on decisions you have already made! This is a particular weak spot for many leaders. How often have you heard (or perhaps even said) the following?

- **'It didn't occur to me.'** People need to be involved in the decisions which affect them. If your team has the chance to influence a decision, they will feel a greater sense of ownership of the outcome than if the decision is taken 'over their heads'.
- **'I didn't have time.'** You might think that you just don't have the time to consult everyone involved. Be warned. The time you will spend later repairing the damage you've caused far outweighs what would have been spent consulting people in the first place!
- **'I knew what was right.'** It's very short-sighted to ignore the wealth of experience and insight of those on your team.

You cannot possibly be in possession of all the facts or ideas on any subject. The more brains there are working on any problem, the better the solution is likely to be.

Remember to:

- **Be respectful:** Always treat the opinions and ideas of others with respect. Never dismiss them out of hand, even if they are weak. If you do, not only will you lose the respect of the person concerned, but they will soon stop volunteering ideas.
- **Watch your language:** It's very easy to be persuaded by each person you talk to, for that moment to see things totally from their perspective and then to make statements that you will later regret. Thank people for their input, and run ideas past them to test their reaction, but make it clear that you need time to consider the overall situation.
- **Consider your church:** It's also very important not to bypass official structures that are in place within your church or organisation. Appropriate groups should always be drawn into your consultation period.

MAKE THE DECISION

Often the decision that is needed won't be the most obvious, or the easiest, one to make. Part of your role as team leader is to 'grasp the nettle'. Bear in mind that:

- If there is no perfect solution, you may have to accept the best of a bad bunch.
- Dithering, procrastinating or opting out never impresses anyone, and will not endear you to your team.
- Once you have reached your decision, you must be committed to it. In fact, the strength of your commitment can often redeem a decision which wasn't the greatest idea to start with.

EXPLAIN THE DECISION

Think through how you are going to explain your decision clearly and persuasively to others. You will only generate enthusiasm in others if you communicate it with clarity and conviction.

If you want others to be committed to a course of action, it is important to explain *why* it has been chosen and *how* it has developed since your consultation with them. Try to think through how you would feel at the receiving end of this information, and anticipate any possible misunderstandings or worries your team might have.

Don't communicate your decision with individuals on an ad-hoc, 'when I bump into them' basis. If the most common complaint in churches is 'nobody ever asked us', the second is 'nobody ever told us'. Unless you think through exactly how you are going to communicate your decision, you run the risk of everyone receiving a different version or interpretation of your message.

Instead, brief all those directly involved in the decision at the same time. When you do this, remember to explain:

- What you have decided
- When the decision will take effect
- Where the changes involved will take place
- How the decision will be implemented
- Who will be affected by it
- Why you have chosen this particular way forward.

Explaining your decision to those involved in this way sends a vital signal. It shows that you value them and appreciate their input. It gives you an important chance to 'nip in the bud' any areas of misunderstanding, and gives your team the chance to ask any questions they might have. Always encourage questions, as they help you to ensure that everybody understands what has been agreed.

MONITOR THE DECISION

Making the decision isn't the end of the process. You now need to monitor the outcome. This will help you smooth out any problems that arise, review how the situation is developing and assess whether the desired results are being achieved. And if you have to modify your decision, or even change course completely, you can do so before a crisis hits!

In conclusion. . .

1. **Teach your team** how to make good decisions. Making decisions is something that your team will be increasingly involved in as you develop your skill at delegating. It is therefore important to show them how to implement this process themselves. Your example will give the lead!

2. **Be accountable** to your team as to how well the decision-making process is being applied. When you meet together, discuss recent decisions – not so much the decisions themselves, but the way they were made and communicated. Lead by asking for feedback, and invite suggestions for improvement.

3. **Support each other** once decisions have been made. This will encourage team loyalty and also keep everyone on their toes!

SECTION 4

Working Together

'Of a good leader, when their work is done,
their aim fulfilled, the people will say:
"We did this ourselves."'
Ancient Chinese proverb

People before projects

In his book *Effective Teambuilding*, management expert John Adair breaks down the work of a team leader into three main areas:

- Achieving the task
- Building and maintaining the team
- Developing the individual.

Simply achieving the task should never be the sole aim of teamwork. The members of your team are not just a means to an end, and the bottom line is not just to get the job done *but also* to enable individuals to develop their full potential.

Some leaders become so absorbed in achieving their goals that they end up oblivious to the effects of their relentless pursuit on those who work with them. The human cost, in terms of quality of life and relationships, appears not to matter as long as the task is achieved. This attitude, often prevalent in business and industry, as well as in the church, has left many people drained of enthusiasm and feeling neglected, ignored and used.

From man to machine

In our society, many people feel dissatisfied and unfulfilled in their work. Part of the reason for this can be traced back to the

Industrial Revolution. Before industrialisation, people were the main source of productivity. Their individual skills were valued, and many could take pride in their work. But when machines were discovered to be more productive and economical, people took a back seat. Factory workers were often no more than an extension of the machines they operated, performing repetitive tasks which left little room for creativity or any uniquely human contribution. The result was frustration, boredom, stress and the loss of human dignity.

Today we have inherited a philosophy of work according to which people can adapt to any job provided the pay is right. Projects and profits are pursued at the expense of individuals, and people's *worth* is often linked to their ability to command a high salary. But God intends people to be fulfilled by their work, not by their pay or economic productivity. We are much more than just a means of production.

In today's economic climate, the church has an enormous opportunity to model a different approach to work, maintaining the value of each individual's contribution in society and helping people derive a sense of satisfaction from what they contribute to others.

Back to basics

If you want your team to function well, the starting point is to be concerned about them as *people*, rather than just with the job they do. If you genuinely care about them, this will be apparent in terms of the *time*, *respect*, *friendship*, *esteem*, *encouragement*, *challenges* and *consideration* you give them. Such concern will improve not only your relationships with them but also their performance. 'Trust men and they will be true to you,' said Emerson. 'Treat them greatly and they will show themselves to be great.'

Give time. Relationship building is a process. Getting to know people takes time and serious commitment. Unless you make it a priority, it will not happen. For any leader, it's too easy to get so caught up in the pressure of personal responsibilities that you end up constantly preoccupied and unavailable to your team. Plan time in your diary to spend with team members, talk to them about what they are doing and how they are finding things. Manage your team by 'being there' for them.

If anyone should have been preoccupied with the task in hand, it was Jesus. But reading the Gospels, you never get the impression that his time with his disciples was squeezed in between public appointments. His disciples were his priority, and he therefore made himself available to them. In fact, in the three years of his recorded ministry, there seems to have been very few times when they weren't around and central to what was going on.

Give respect. To give respect requires the right attitude. Because the decisions they constantly have to make inevitably affect and shape the lives of others, it's easy for leaders to consider themselves more important than those around them. Once such an attitude gets hold, it is bound to surface in the way a person relates to others. It will tend to come across in the unconscious little things they say, as well as in those things they don't bother to say.

If you respect your team, it will show itself in the way you encourage members to express their individuality and listen to their views and opinions. Remember, your team will only give you their honest thoughts if they are sure you really want to know, and that you will not hold it against them if and when they disagree with you.

Give friendship. 'Not only is friendship compatible with the biblical model of leadership, it is an integral part of it,' says Tom Marshall. It requires you to relate to your team as *equals*. Friends are consciously and deliberately on the same level, regardless of their status or position. They are open with one another and admit their weaknesses. If you are a friend to your team, you will keep close to them.

Jesus was not a leader who held himself aloof, or kept a distance that might have been considered appropriate for the 'Son of God'! He called his disciples his friends, and confided in them. The key to his whole ministry was that of *incarnation* – he got involved. One of the last times he appeared to his disciples, we find him cooking breakfast for them on the beach – hardly the most stately way to herald his resurrection!

Give esteem. In George Bernard Shaw's play, *Pygmalion*, Eliza Doolittle explains: 'The difference between a lady and a flower girl is not how she behaves, but how she is treated. I shall always be a flower girl to Professor Higgins, because he always treats me as a flower girl, and always will, but I know I can be a lady to you, because you always treat me as a lady, and always will.'

Contrary to popular opinion, it is impossible to develop a high level of self-esteem and confidence without the help of others. The image we have of ourselves is created by the way other people respond to us. Poor self-image, so prevalent today, is the result of not being esteemed or appreciated by others. Parents, partners, teachers, friends, employers, and sometimes even church leaders, all play their part.

Every person has intrinsic value because they were created by God for a purpose. This value has nothing to do with their performance or merit. When Jesus was baptised – before he had even begun his public life and ministry – God said, 'This is my Son, with whom I am pleased.' Giving someone value or esteem means treating them in a way that says, 'You are an important part of this team because of who you are.' If their value as a person is not clearly established, or if the value of their performance gets over-emphasised, then they will feel valuable only when they are achieving. Even the slightest failure can then become a crippling experience for them.

The best way for an individual to improve their self-esteem is to learn to see themselves as God sees them, and to develop an appreciation of the value he attaches to them. As a team leader, you play a key role in creating, encouraging and reinforcing this understanding.

Give encouragement. You can increase the self-confidence of your team members further by drawing attention to their strengths and abilities. Appreciating their unique qualities will increase their sense of belonging. Everyone has some skill or attribute worth praising. Make sure that you recognise team members' achievements both publicly and privately. Don't make the mistake of speaking highly of people only to third parties – remember to say good things to their face. And don't condemn them with half-hearted or faint praise. We all thrive on praise and recognition, which means that team members who are treated positively will be motivated to do even better in the future.

Give challenges. Asking someone to do something challenging is another way of expressing a high opinion of their abilities. You are investing your trust in an unproven ability, placing your confidence in them, and taking a risk. To get the best out of someone, you have to make sure they are constantly challenged by their role. Once a person can fulfil their task without it stretching them, their interest in it will wane. Your team will never give their best if they are bored.

If team members fail in a task, don't automatically write them off. Allow them to fail, but don't let them get away with a level of performance that is below what you *know* they can achieve. Believing and expecting the very best of them, and helping them to find ways to improve, will encourage them to expect the best of themselves.

Give consideration. Bear in mind that team members have a life outside the team. How many Christians do you know who are disillusioned with the church because they or their partners have been 'bled dry' by task-obsessed leaders? It is important to be interested in their wider world. What's happening to your team at home and at work? What problems are they facing at the moment? When are their birthdays? What are their hobbies? Give them your time and prove that you don't take them for granted.

Question time

How much do you value your team? They will instinctively know by the things you say and the way you act. What would you do in the following situations?

1. A team member arrives for a pre-arranged meeting to talk to you about a difficulty. Do you:
   (a) Sit with a pile of work in front of you and talk to them between phone calls and other interruptions? ☐
   (b) Apologise for interruptions but still deal with them (after all, they appreciate how busy you are)? ☐
   (c) Put everything aside, make sure that you are not interrupted and that they know that they have your complete attention? ☐

2. Another church has written to say how much they have appreciated your team's involvement on a recent occasion, but you know they could have done much better. Do you:
   (a) Say nothing, because telling them about the letter could go to their heads and encourage them to settle for low standards? ☐
   (b) Tell your team what was said, but make it clear they could do better, and offer suggested improvements? ☐
   (c) Tell them what was said and find at least *one* positive comment on each individual's input? Ask for their own opinion on their performance, and draw out from this some possible improvements? ☐

3. Your team are going out together for a meal, and have invited you to join them. Do you:

   (a) Decline, although you have no prior engagement? Your time would be better spent on more important matters. ☐

   (b) Go, to show your support, but constantly check your watch and make a get-away as soon as you think it's acceptable? ☐

   (c) Go, and *enjoy* yourself – informal times are great ways to build and strengthen friendships, which improve team 'dynamics'? ☐

4. A team member with little self-confidence has missed the agreed deadline for giving you a report. It's not actually essential for you to have it for another week. Do you:

   (a) Give them another week, but make sure that they know they have let you down? ☐

   (b) Tell them not to worry about it, that you don't actually need it for another week, and that you feel sure they are doing their best? ☐

   (c) Find out why they haven't done it, give them another week, but arrange time to discuss what went wrong and how they could manage better in future? ☐

SCORE ANALYSIS

Mainly 'a's: If you *could* do everything yourself you probably would. If you value your team, they are unlikely to recognise it. Talk this issue through further with another leader you respect.

Mainly 'b's: You value your team – you just need a little encouragement to show it more clearly. Work hard at focusing on their strengths and list one practical way of showing you appreciate each member of your team in a public way.

Mainly 'c's: If your team don't feel good about themselves yet, they soon will. Make sure their work is challenging, because they are likely to rise to the challenges you set them.

Training for success

Successful people are always those who know or have discovered what their strengths are, and spend the rest of their life getting better and better at what they are already good at doing.   Tom Marshall

Everybody is good at *something*. God has created each of us with a purpose, and gives us what we need to achieve it. We are usually naturally motivated towards the things we do best, and when involved in these tasks we find enjoyment and satisfaction, and produce our best work.

As a leader, you have the challenge and opportunity to help people find fulfilment by:

- Knowing your team
- Matching their gifts to tasks
- Providing relevant training.

Time spent in these pursuits will be time well spent.

Knowing your team

Skills take time and effort to develop, but they should grow out of natural *gifts and abilities*. Some people are very aware of their abilities while others haven't got a clue. You should spend time with each member of your team discussing what their gifts are.

Many people find it difficult to verbalise what their strengths are, either through lack of awareness or because of the fear of sounding big-headed. So rather than asking them what they are good at, the best approach is to start by chatting over the sort of things they *enjoy* doing, and their achievements in these areas.

Make a list of the specific tasks they enjoy, as well as more general abilities like organising, planning, leading, teaching or research. Don't be too concerned at this stage about how their abilities relate to the work of the team. It's important also to talk about *why* they enjoy particular tasks and to understand their *personality*. For instance, is a team member the pioneering type who enjoys taking risks and thrives on new challenges? Are they more cautious – do they like to make sure that a job is organised and done well? Do they enjoy analysing, researching and investigating the best approach for a task? Or are they in their element when dealing with people, helping to ensure that a project runs smoothly?

Remember that while there are different degrees of gifting, everyone has some ability and people with few skills might not have unearthed their gifts yet – so be prepared to do a bit of digging if necessary!

Having got this far, now it's your job to think through how each individual member of your team learns best. Some people will find it easiest to understand if you present something conceptually, while others might struggle with concepts until they are proven by experience. Some people are more inclined to an analytical approach and learn best by working through all the implications while others like things well earthed and defined. Find out what *learning style* is best suited to each of your team members.

Each person also needs a different *leadership style* to bring out the best in them. Find out which style is best suited to each of the members of your team. Once a goal is defined, do they like specific instructions on how to achieve a task or do they prefer to decide themselves? Do they thrive on pressure or buckle under it? Would they like you to give them a lot of freedom or consistent, regular assistance? Do they enjoy being in charge or playing a more supportive role? What would they value most from you as a leader?

Make the effort to adapt yourself to the style best suited to each person. Remember there is always more than one way of doing something. Don't take the arrogant attitude that your preferred style must be the best, and that you would merely be pandering to their weaknesses by changing. A little flexibility on your part will create the climate for each member to give their best.

Matching gifts to tasks

The next stage is to give people tasks appropriate to their gifts and abilities. Make sure you *build on strengths*, not work on weaknesses. Though your team may not have had the opportunity of gaining experience in the specific areas required, this in itself does not necessarily present a problem. Make use of their natural attitudes and aptitudes and focus on their potential.

But beware of pigeon-holing people. If someone makes it clear that they would like the opportunity to try their hand at something new, if at all possible encourage them to do so by creating the opening for them. It's often not until a person is given the opportunity of trying something that you discover whether or not they are suited to it.

Providing relevant training

It's your job to ensure that each member of your team receives the encouragement, opportunities, resources and support required to develop their gifts and achieve their tasks. Don't just leave them to sink or swim! When help is needed, can your team members be sure of your understanding, compassionate and practical response?

Effective learning is the result of a creative combination of formal training and practical experience, which is something known as 'praxis'. The study of books and the attendance of relevant courses and seminars is vital, but of little long-term value without lots of practical experience. Two equal and opposite errors are commonly made, particularly in areas of training for church leadership. One is the belief that before you do a job, you have to go on an intensive training course and have your ability proved by a diploma or certificate. The second is the belief that there is no value in formal education and that it's better just to leave people to get on with a job, hoping that they learn as they go. A balance between theory and the experience which reinforces it is always the best approach. *Theory and practice belong hand in hand*.

Your aim should be to put people into situations which will motivate them to develop their skills as well as reinforce formal training. Suppose that one of your youth team is asked a question they cannot answer. They will then be motivated to find out the answer and get back to the enquirer; and in the process they will probably remember the point. Seminars and books alone provide little motivation to retain information, no experience to reinforce it and ultimately no fulfilment.

Jesus provided the ultimate model for training a team. During their three-year 'intensive training course', Jesus' disciples watched what he did, asked lots of questions, worked alongside him, had the chance to experiment, were allowed to make *plenty* of mistakes without fear of being condemned, and were then sent off to replicate his work, with the promise 'You will do greater things than me.'

Tough love

In order to train your team for success it is vital that you help them develop *self-discipline*. Unfortunately, for many of us, the word 'criticism' has connotations of being 'told off' when we've done something wrong. It's regarded in a wholly negative light because the majority of criticism we have experienced has come from people who had little real concern for us or commitment to us.

Constructive criticism is about training people to face up to and 'own' the consequences of their actions, and creating a framework which will encourage self-discipline. This can only happen in the context of a relationship where a team member knows that you have their best interests at heart; your motivation is that you truly want their success to outshine yours. Tom Landry, manager of the Dallas Cowboys, has said, 'My job as coach is to make people do what they don't want to do, so that they can achieve what they want to achieve.'

Discipline is sometimes regarded as the enemy of freedom. It is your job to show your team that the reverse is true. Discipline is the route to freedom. Freedom is the end reward of discipline. For instance, the freedom of a great musician to express themselves through their instrument is born of hours and hours of disciplined rehearsal. The pianist who avoids the discipline of daily practice will never experience the freedom of fingers that dance across the keys and create music that is a delight to the ears! If your team know that you genuinely believe in them and their future, they will be much more inclined to accept sensitive correction and constructive criticism when it is necessary.

Life after the team

If you're doing your job well, there normally comes a time for individuals within your team to move on to new things. They need to be released by you to allow them to develop further and face new challenges. Perhaps they should now even be leading a team of their own. Never let the needs of your team stand in the way of its members' personal progress. Remember that the ultimate aim is to see each person fulfilled and their potential maximised, not stunted by the limitations of the opportunities their present role offers. It's always hard to let go but in the end it's best for you and your team as well as for the individual concerned.

Understanding conflict

Learning to confront and to handle disagreement constructively is a vital expression of genuine care. It is another difficult but essential skill for team leaders, though one that Christians have often neglected. Perhaps to acknowledge our difficulties in this area would be to admit our failure to be 'truly spiritual'. As a result, the church's response to disagreement within its ranks has often been to push it under the carpet and pray for it to disappear.

Another approach is that of attempting to cover up problems by resorting to singing worship songs about love being 'shared among us', etc, while grinning at each other and holding hands in a circle. But while the sentiments may be genuine, gazing lovingly into each other's eyes is no long-term solution to conflict and tension.

It's natural that disagreements should arise in the life of any church from time to time. A close look at the New Testament will reveal plenty of tension in the life of the early church. At different times, for instance, Paul has major disputes with Barnabas, Peter, and the whole Jerusalem Council. The big question is how you choose to deal with it.

When a team member has a disagreement with someone else, either inside or outside the team, it can slowly erode morale, with everyone involved inevitably suffering. The leader who, through weakness or 'nicety', fails to confront disagreement and deal with it quickly, simply stores up trouble for the future. Unchecked tension grows rather than vanishes, and the eventual outcome is always destructive.

In order to deal effectively with conflict, it's essential first to understand the underlying causes. Follow the four steps below to help you in that task.

(1) Anticipate the problems

Whenever possible, your aim should be to deal with disagreement *before* it boils over and develops into open or heated conflict.

- Be alert. Make it a priority to keep in touch with the current feelings and opinions of others.
- Avoid the temptation to 'opt out' and let things drift when you are aware of disagreements or problems, or a clashing of opinions or personalities. You are the leader, and it is your responsibility to resolve conflicts before they explode whenever you can.

(2) Identify the stakeholders

A 'stakeholder' in any disagreement is someone with a stake in the issues concerned. This could, of course, include you. The list of stakeholders is made up not only of the main characters in the dispute, but also includes anyone likely to be concerned with its outcome – both those who have to implement decisions and those who have to live with them.

(3) Clarify the issues

In order to deal with conflict, you first need to diagnose the situation effectively. Never assume that you know all the facts, or that your initial impression is accurate. Get honest feedback from all those involved. Their perspective may be very different from yours, and could introduce you to valuable insights and information that you would otherwise have missed.

- **Focus on issues not personalities.** Don't be drawn into shifting the focus of attention from the issues to the personalities involved. And remember never to fall into the trap of making derogatory or demeaning comments. These dangers are especially acute if you are personally involved in the conflict! Do your best to protect the dignity of *everyone* involved, and resist the temptation to put others down, even when you regard their views as stubborn or stupid. Your task is to do all you can to mend strained or broken relationships, and to build self-esteem whenever possible – not to have the opposite effect.

- **Listen with empathy.** Attempt to put yourself in the shoes of each person involved in the disagreement, and to see things from their perspective. Your attitude and behaviour will determine how much you are told, and what kind of reception you get. If you appear judgemental or condemnatory, you will end up getting the shutters pulled down on you. If you ask for honest feedback, don't react negatively when you receive it. Always remember that the most powerful key to influencing the attitude and behaviour of others is the way that you relate to them, not the strength of your argument.

(4) Assess the sources of disagreement

Did the dispute arise:

- Because of inaccurate or incomplete information held by someone involved? If so, how can you ensure that the situation is effectively remedied as soon as possible?
- Because those involved hold to differing methods, goals, aims or principles? If so, is there a higher level at which all the stakeholders share a common vision? If common ground on which agreement already exists can be identified, this can be used as a foundation on which to build a way forward.

- Because of different perceptions of the present situation? If so, remember that what one person sees as a challenge or opportunity, another may regard as a problem or threat.
- As the result of lingering resentment carried over from previously unresolved issues and conflicts? People who have felt betrayed, put down or neglected often act in punishing ways to even up the score. When disagreements stem from old wounds, they can be hard to diagnose. Those involved rarely acknowledge the real problem, even if they are aware of it. Is there a way in which these can be uncovered, confronted and dealt with? Also remember that someone who is antagonistic towards an individual may actually be working out their resentment or negative feelings towards your whole team, the church, or themselves.

By working through these four steps, you will begin to get a more objective understanding of the root causes and basic issues behind any disagreement within or faced by your team.

REAL-LIFE CRISIS

- Think of a recent disagreement in which you have been involved, or one that is developing within your team, and write down a brief description of it, including the factors and general situation that led up to it.

- Write down the names of all those people with a vested interest in the outcome of events.

- Write down the central issues in the disagreement.

- Write down your personal assessment of the sources of the disagreement, including your view of how long they have been brewing.

Resolving conflict

Once you are armed with a clear understanding of the *causes* of a disagreement or conflict, you are in a good position to set about *resolving* it. When relationship or performance problems do arise, it's very important that, as the team leader, you are seen to act swiftly and decisively. Problems which are not confronted early soon become issues that affect the whole team.

Choosing your response

Every professional golfer has a full set of clubs at their disposal. But they must choose the most appropriate one for each shot. Only a fool would choose the same club every time just because it was their favourite!

Similarly, to deal with disagreement effectively and to prevent destructive conflict, a skilled leader needs a whole range of problem-solving approaches in their repertoire. Like the golfer choosing the right club, the skill of any leader is to choose the appropriate course of action for each problem. The leader who claims, 'This is how I *always* deal with problems. . .' is headed for disaster. Whether their style of confrontation is aggressive, apologetic or non-existent, they are no different from the golfer who insists on playing their shot with a no. 9 iron whether it's a six-inch putt or a 300-yard drive!

There is no *one* universally applicable conflict-resolving approach that is always guaranteed to do the job. Your task, as a good leader, is to become familiar with as wide a variety of methods as possible, and then to develop the ability to choose the right one at the right time. It is, however, vital that *you* choose your course of action, rather than allowing circumstances to force your hand and dictate your response.

Getting it right

The basic question you should always ask is: how flexible should I be? Some situations need extreme firmness, while others require a softer approach. The methods of dealing with disagreement and conflict fall into three basic categories.

SOFT

This approach is one of **acceptance**. It involves accepting both sides of the argument and allowing both sets of views and opinions to exist alongside one another. This approach might at first be mistaken for weakness, but it may prove to be the best way forward in some circumstances. You might, for instance, have higher-priority issues to deal with, or need more time to collect information, build rapport, let emotions cool or allow recent changes to stabilise before taking another stance.

Example: In 1 Corinthians 8, Paul addresses the conflict which had arisen about whether or not it was right to eat meat that had been offered to idols. He said people were free to act according to their conscience, but that if one person's freedom created a problem for someone else they should refrain. Basically he was accepting both viewpoints because there were more important things to be concerned about.

FLEXIBLE

This approach is one of **collaboration**. It involves co-operation between parties, with give and take on all sides. Those involved in the dispute commit themselves to sitting down and listening to each other, so that through frank and honest discussion, they can develop a mutually acceptable solution. In reality, this approach can only be taken if all participants in the discussion are trustworthy, capable and willing to communicate with each other.

Example: In Acts 15, we read that Paul and Barnabas were brought into 'sharp dispute and debate' with the council at Jerusalem over the issue of whether Gentile believers should be subject to Jewish laws. After 'much discussion' a consensus was reached.

HARD

This approach is one of **domination**, where an attempt is made unilaterally to use power and influence to gain total compliance. Domination can be appropriate when speed of action is *absolutely essential*, but using it unwisely can be very destructive.

Example: On various occasions Paul told local churches to exclude people who were causing serious problems. He felt that certain issues were so important to the life of the church that such drastic action was essential.

The conflict resolution checklist

How do you choose the right course of action? Is the correct approach hard or soft? How firm or flexible should you aim to be?

Having assessed your 'Real-Life Crisis' in the last section, now choose an appropriate course of action. Check that you've made a wise choice by answering the following questions:

	YES	PROBABLY	UNLIKELY
Will my chosen course of action advance the goals of the team?	☐	☐	☐

Will my chosen course of
action be acceptable to others
involved?   ☐   ☐   ☐
Will my chosen course of
action result in greater benefits
and fewer drawbacks than the
alternatives?   ☐   ☐   ☐

If all three answers are in the 'yes' column, you should feel confident to pursue the course of action you have in mind.

If you have any ticks in the 'probably' column, you should give the pros and cons of your proposed action some further serious thought, carefully considering a more flexible approach before making a final decision.

If you have any ticks in the 'unlikely' column, do not proceed. Rethink your approach. The cost of your proposed action is likely to be considerable, both in terms of relationships and of your team goals.

Building commitment

Commitment can never be forced. Any attempt you make to coerce or pressurise others into it is doomed to failure and is likely to produce exactly the opposite effect. Building commitment from others is a process that takes time and a great deal of sensitivity on your part. But as it develops, it results in a deepening sense of corporate 'ownership' of the team's vision, as well as increasing loyalty between members and an inclination to put team interests before personal ones.

The strongest team is built when its members are committed *to the task*, *to each other* and *to the team* unit. The wise leader is one who works hard to develop these three aspects of team life.

(1) Committed to the task

Although each member needs their own clearly defined role within the team, it's important to encourage their commitment to its overall goal. Building this kind of overall commitment can be done in a number of ways:

- **Involve team members in setting objectives.** Your team members will come to you with some initial commitment to the overall vision of the team. Your task is actively to involve them in planning the strategy designed to realise this vision, which will both deepen and strengthen their commitment to it. Shared responsibility for results always turns team objectives into *our* objectives.

- **Lead by example.** If you are naturally enthusiastic about your team's purpose, and see tasks not as necessary duties but as exciting challenges, then your team will probably share your attitude. Remember that every obstacle and problem is actually a carefully disguised opportunity.

- **Value their individual contribution.** It's important that each individual always understands how their particular task fits into the wider team context and plays its part in achieving the overall goal. If team members don't have this information or understanding, their commitment level will drop.

(2) Committed to each other

If individuals are committed to the task, they will find it easier to be committed to one another. Shared interests always provide a foundation for good relationships.

- **Build friendship.** Genuine friendship takes time to build, but is essential for strong personal commitment. Concern for each other's interests will help to provide the patience and trust required when things get tough or mistakes are made. As Paul said, *'Love covers over a multitude of sins'* (1 Pet 4:8).

- **Model loyalty.** Make sure that you are always loyal to your team. When individuals fail, don't fall into the trap of running them down publicly, or in front of each other. You cannot expect more from them than you are willing to give. As a result of your loyalty to them, your team will find it easier to treat one another the same way.

(3) Committed to the team

A team is much more than a group of individuals working on different tasks to achieve a common goal. Belonging to your team should be a fulfilling and meaningful experience in itself for each of the members. You can encourage commitment to the team as a *unit* in a number of ways.

- **Provide information.** Be as 'open' as possible with your team members. If you don't keep them informed, they will feel left out, unimportant and frustrated. Some leaders tend to guard information like trade secrets to protect their power. But knowledge, like power, is most productive when given away. Other leaders simply 'forget' to tell their team what's happening because they don't think it's important or because they are disorganised in their communication. Without information, your team won't know what's going on in the big picture, what progress is being made, what difficulties are being faced, or how they can best help. Sharing as much information as possible and confiding in your team (without gossiping or breaking confidences) will encourage their help, advice and ideas, as well as their involvement and commitment.

- **Schedule regular meetings.** Meeting together regularly will help your team to appreciate each other's responsibilities, skills, depth of commitment and struggles. People who understand and respect each other will find it easier to identify as a team. Individual problems become team problems, and team members are more likely to support and cover for each other when difficulties arise. As a leader, it's up to you to ensure that team meetings are well organised, focused and productive. Don't allow them to ramble aimlessly. Ensure that everyone has the opportunity to express their views and opinions. Conversation should not just be 'one-way traffic' consisting of you talking and the team listening. It should be multi-directional, everyone talking to each other.

- **Talk 'team'.** The language we use expresses our attitude. Encourage your team through your example by actually talking 'team'. Always refer to *our* team rather than *my* team. When talking to those outside the team, talk about what 'we' are doing, about 'our' goal, etc. This kind of phraseology is absolutely crucial in building a sense of team commitment.

- **Celebrate success.** Never underestimate the powerful effect of recognising a job well done. Celebrating achievement is a great way to show people your appreciation, as well as to continue to build commitment. Just as when difficulties arise everyone shares the responsibility, so when the team does well everyone should share the credit.

Close the commitment gap

Have you ever said (or thought), 'The problem with my team is their lack of commitment'? If so, then go back through this section and pick out your three weakest points. Decide what positive steps you are going to take to improve your performance in these areas and start today.

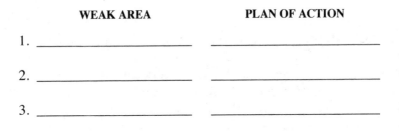

	WEAK AREA	PLAN OF ACTION
1.	_____	_____
2.	_____	_____
3.	_____	_____

SECTION 5

Time to Act

Review time

It would be very easy, having read this book, simply to shelve it. Perhaps it has confirmed things you already understood about team leadership, reminded you of weak spots on which you ought to brush up and even given you a few new insights to chew over. But unless you make a real commitment to act on your response it will all have been a waste of your time. It is essential that you DO SOMETHING NOW.

Putting it off until a later date means that this book is doomed to join the huge pile already waiting on your shelf to be actioned at a time that never comes.

The last section of *Making a Team Work* is designed to help you develop an 'action plan' tailored to your particular needs. But first it's important that you assess your areas of strength and weakness as a team leader in order to decide where to concentrate your efforts. The following questionnaire reviews the material covered in sections two to four of *Making a Team Work*. Answer the questions in each section honestly by circling the appropriate number from 1 to 5.

Score 5 – if you're excellent in that area
4 – if you're reasonably strong
3 – if you're average
2 – if you're fairly weak
1 – if you're pretty useless

Section 2 Review

QUALITIES OF AN EFFECTIVE TEAM LEADER

Clear vision

1. I have a long-term plan	5 4 3 2 1
2. I am excited about future possibilities.	5 4 3 2 1
3. I am clear about my team's purpose and direction.	5 4 3 2 1
4. I am open to new ideas and ways of doing things.	5 4 3 2 1
5. I enjoy talking about my plans.	5 4 3 2 1

TOTAL: _____

The willingness to delegate

1. I don't hold on to work simply because I'm good at it and I enjoy it.	5 4 3 2 1
2. I try to concentrate on planning, organising and motivating rather than doing tasks others could manage.	5 4 3 2 1
3. I am willing to take calculated risks by trusting others with tasks which I know I could perform myself.	5 4 3 2 1
4. I place a high priority on spending time training my team.	5 4 3 2 1
5. I am not constantly concerned about asking too much of my team members.	5 4 3 2 1

TOTAL: _____

The use of power

1. I lead because it seems to be the best way I can serve.   5 4 3 2 1
2. I keep close to my team and enjoy being with the individual members.   5 4 3 2 1
3. I don't consider any task 'below' my status as a leader.   5 4 3 2 1
4. I am genuinely pleased when others do well, and do not feel my position threatened by their success.   5 4 3 2 1
5. I put the best interests of those I lead before my own.   5 4 3 2 1

TOTAL: _____

Trustworthiness

1. When I say I am going to do something, I do it. People know they can rely on me.   5 4 3 2 1
2. I am open with people and do not reshape or edit the truth according to my audience. They all get the same story.   5 4 3 2 1
3. I don't break confidences.   5 4 3 2 1
4. Those I lead know they can depend on my loyalty to them in all circumstances.   5 4 3 2 1
5. When things get tough, I don't whinge or criticise other people.   5 4 3 2 1

TOTAL: ____

Accountability

1. Other leaders I respect have a definite say in what I do.   5 4 3 2 1
2. I have made myself accountable to my team and am happy to deal with any questions they raise about my leadership.   5 4 3 2 1
3. I am willing to shoulder the responsibility if mistakes are made by my team.   5 4 3 2 1

4. I am willing to reconsider my course of
   action if those to whom I am accountable
   think it necessary.   5 4 3 2 1
5. I am constantly aware of my responsibility
   to maximise the talents and opportunities
   God has given me.   5 4 3 2 1

                                              TOTAL: _____

List results

Now list the qualities covered in this first section of the questionnaire from your weakest to your strongest area.

1. _____ (Weakest)

2. _____

3. _____

4. _____

5. _____ (Strongest)

Section 3 Review

SKILLS OF TEAM LEADERSHIP

Communicating and motivating

1. I usually receive a positive response to any presentation I do.   5 4 3 2 1
2. I make a point of checking that people have understood what I have said.   5 4 3 2 1
3. I can recruit volunteers when I need them.   5 4 3 2 1
4. I am totally committed to my team's goals(s) and everyone knows it.   5 4 3 2 1
5. When someone joins my team, they know they are in for what will be a challenging but enjoyable time.   5 4 3 2 1

TOTAL: _____

Choosing your team

1. I tend to focus on people's potential rather than their weaknesses.   5 4 3 2 1
2. I take the time to get to know people before I make a decision about team membership.   5 4 3 2 1
3. I consider whether a person's involvement on a team would be in their best interests.   5 4 3 2 1
4. I enjoy the challenge of recruiting unlikely candidates.   5 4 3 2 1
5. I consider the overall balance when forming a team.   5 4 3 2 1

TOTAL: _____

Goals and objectives

1. I have specific long-term goal(s) for my
   team and a clear strategy of how to get
   there.   5 4 3 2 1
2. My team are involved in setting our
   objectives and planning our strategy.   5 4 3 2 1
3. We meet regularly as a team to assess our
   progress.   5 4 3 2 1
4. My team members also have clear
   individual objectives.   5 4 3 2 1
5. Our goal(s) and objectives are written down,
   down, measurable, attainable, challenging
   and timed.   5 4 3 2 1

TOTAL: _____

Delegation

1. I spend my time planning, organising,
   motivating and overseeing, rather than
   doing the tasks others could do.   5 4 3 2 1
2. When I delegate, I give careful
   consideration as to who would benefit the
   most from the task and the responsibility
   involved.   5 4 3 2 1
3. I delegate work which will give team
   members the opportunity to develop their
   gifts.   5 4 3 2 1
4. When I delegate, I explain the task
   carefully, share all the information I have,
   and make myself available for feedback
   and support.   5 4 3 2 1
5. As team members become more competent,
   I give them greater freedom and
   responsibility.   5 4 3 2 1

TOTAL: _____

Making decisions

1. Before making a decision, I make sure
   that I have the relevant information, and
   am not pressured into premature action.   5 4 3 2 1
2. I make time to listen to the opinions of all
   those whose lives the decision will affect. 5 4 3 2 1
3. I do not opt out of making decisions when
   circumstances are difficult.   5 4 3 2 1
4. I communicate my decisions clearly to all
   those affected.   5 4 3 2 1
5. Having made a decision, I monitor it, and
   am willing to modify it if necessary.   5 4 3 2 1

TOTAL: _____

List results

Now list the qualities covered in this first section of the questionnaire from your weakest to your strongest area.

1. _____ (Weakest)

2. _____

3. _____

4. _____

5. _____ (Strongest)

Section 4 Review

WORKING TOGETHER

People before projects

1. I make the time to get to know my team –
   they know I am interested in them.   5 4 3 2 1
2. I respect my team. They know I will not
   hold it against them if they raise questions. 5 4 3 2 1
3. I appreciate my team, and regularly tell
   them so, both publicly and privately.   5 4 3 2 1
4. I bear in mind an individual's
   commitments outside the team, and do not
   pressure them unduly.   5 4 3 2 1
5. I believe in my team and therefore expect
   expect the best from them, so I make sure
   that they find their work with me
   challenging.   5 4 3 2 1

                                       TOTAL: _____

Training for success

1. I give time to understanding my team
   members' personalities and to discovering
   their natural abilities.   5 4 3 2 1
2. When I delegate I aim to develop natural
   abilities.   5 4 3 2 1
3. I encourage my team members to
   experiment with new areas of
   responsibility and hold back
   from pigeon-holing them.   5 4 3 2 1
4. I make sure all my team members
   receive adequate training for their
   tasks.   5 4 3 2 1

5. I am willing to adapt my leadership style
to draw out the best from each individual
team member.   5 4 3 2 1

TOTAL: _____

Understanding conflict

1. I work hard to keep in touch with the
feelings and opinions of my team.   5 4 3 2 1
2. When a disagreement occurs, I don't jump
to conclusions but instead seek to clarify
issues by getting honest feedback from all
those involved.   5 4 3 2 1
3. I remain objective, and focus on issues
rather than allowing myself to be side-
tracked by the personalities involved.   5 4 3 2 1
4. I am good at recognising the
'stakeholders' in a dispute.   5 4 3 2 1
5. I set out to discover the root causes of
both how and why a dispute has arisen.   5 4 3 2 1

TOTAL: _____

Resolving conflict

1. As soon as I'm aware of a disagreement, I
take action. I don't opt out or just hope
that it will resolve itself in time.   5 4 3 2 1
2. I have a range of different approaches to
dealing with conflict within the team.   5 4 3 2 1
3. I have a good understanding of when to
use which approach.   5 4 3 2 1
4. I take the initiative as to which approach I
use and am not controlled by other people
or circumstances.   5 4 3 2 1
5. When resolving conflict my aim is to ensure
that my course of action will advance the
overall goals and morale of my team.   5 4 3 2 1

TOTAL: _____

Building commitment

1. Each of my team members has a clear
   understanding of how their particular task
   and role fits into the 'big picture'.   5 4 3 2 1
2. My team are friends as well as colleagues,
   and enjoy working together.   5 4 3 2 1
3. I am loyal to my team members, and do
   not become critical of them when the
   going gets tough.   5 4 3 2 1
4. We all place high priority on being at
   regular team meetings.   5 4 3 2 1
5. We take the time to relax together and
   celebrate our successes.   5 4 3 2 1

                                      TOTAL: _____

List results

Now list the qualities covered in this section of the questionnaire
from your weakest to your strongest area.

1. _____ (Weakest)

2. _____

3. _____

4. _____

5. _____ (Strongest)

Decision time

Go back and **highlight one aspect** in each of the three sections
which you would like to make it a priority to develop. It will
probably be the one for which you scored lowest, but may also
depend on your particular circumstances and which qualities are
really crucial to you. But remember it's also good to take notice
of and be encouraged by your areas of strength!

An action plan

The last step is to make a definite commitment to work at improving your team building and leadership skills by developing an action plan. You might want to tackle one area from each of the three sections of the questionnaire, or choose to concentrate all your efforts on qualities, skills, or aspects of working together. It might suit you more to tackle a different area every six months. Do whatever is most appropriate to you and your circumstances.

Six steps to positive action

Use the following six steps to develop your plan.

1. **Quality, skill or aspect of working together.** Write down the area(s) you have decided to work on.

2. **Your goal.** Be specific. Statements like 'To be more worthy of trust' are far too general and almost impossible to measure progress on. It's more realistic and practical to set yourself a goal such as 'aiming to invest ongoing trust in three team members over the next six weeks'.

3. **The obstacles.** Consider the barriers you will need to overcome in order to achieve your goal. These could include your own lack of knowledge, discipline, motivation, resources or training necessary. Existing time pressures might also present

a problem. Once you identify the obstacles, you can begin planning how to overcome them.

4. Your strategy. How will you overcome these obstacles and achieve your goal? What objectives should you plan in order to reach your goal? What help do you need and where will you find it?

5. The timetable. Set a date by which you plan to achieve your goal, as well as those for your interim objectives. Also plan at this stage to monitor and review your progress regularly.

6. Accountability. Accountability to others provides great help and motivation. Think of someone who demonstrates the quality or skill you want to develop. Ask if they would be willing to help you in this area. Go over your action plan with them. Plan to meet at regular intervals to monitor your progress.

1. QUALITY: _____

2. GOAL: _____

_____

3. OBSTACLES: _____

_____

4. STRATEGY: _____

_____

5. TIMETABLE: _____

_____

6. ACCOUNTABLE TO: _____

Checkpoint

Is this goal: Specific? .... ☐

Measurable? .... ☐

Attainable? .... ☐

Challenging? .... ☐

Timed? .... ☐

1. SKILL: _____

2. GOAL: _____

_____

3. OBSTACLES: _____

_____

4. STRATEGY: _____

_____

5. TIMETABLE: _____

_____

6. ACCOUNTABLE TO: _____

Checkpoint

Is this goal: Specific? .... ☐

Measurable? .... ☐

Attainable? .... ☐

Challenging? .... ☐

Timed? .... ☐

1. TEAM SKILL: _____

2. GOAL: _____

_____

3. OBSTACLES: _____

_____

4. STRATEGY: _____

_____

5. TIMETABLE: _____

_____

6. ACCOUNTABLE TO: _____

Checkpoint

Is this goal: Specific? .... ☐

Measurable? .... ☐

Attainable? .... ☐

Challenging? .... ☐

Timed? .... ☐

LIGHT FOR LIGHTBEARERS

ALPHA magazine, helps you to listen to the word of God and hear the cry of the world, so that you can be a light to the world:

◆STEVE CHALKE - each month he explores aspects of faith in his hard hitting column.

◆NEWS - how the Church is responding to contemporary issues

◆CULTURE - reviews of books, films and music that are shaping the church and the world

◆INSIGHT - in-depth balanced examination of hot-potato issues such as Education, Homosexuality, Divorce, Deliverance, and other topical debates

◆TRENDS - why is religious classical music so popular? What is God doing on the information superhighway?

◆FOUNDATIONS - Every month you'll discover fresh insights into Worship, Evangelism, Leadership, Small Groups, Prayer and Life in the Workplace.

No-one else offers such consistent, quality insights.

DISCOVER ALPHA TODAY FOR FREE.

Fill in the coupon below and post it to us and we'll send you a sample copy of ALPHA. We will also tell you how to obtain it regularly from your nearest Christian bookshop or subscribe and have it delivered to your door.

NAME: _____

ADDRESS:_____

_____

POST CODE:_____